W9-AOT-839

COWBOYS
AND
DRAGONS

**SHATTERING CULTURAL MYTHS TO
ADVANCE CHINESE-AMERICAN BUSINESS**

CHARLES LEE, PH.D.

Dearborn™
Trade Publishing
A **Kaplan Professional** Company

Vice President and Publisher: Cynthia A. Zigmund
Editorial Director: Donald J. Hull
Senior Acquisitions Editor: Jean Iversen
Senior Project Editor: Trey Thoelcke
Interior Design: Lucy Jenkins
Cover Design: Jody Billert
Typesetting: Elizabeth Pitts

© 2003 by Charles Lee

Published by Dearborn Trade Publishing, a Kaplan Professional Company

Printed in the United States of America

03 04 05 10 9 8 7 6 5 4 3 2 1

Library of Congress Cataloging-in-Publication Data

Lee, Charles (Charles Tsungnan), 1940-
    Cowboys and dragons : shattering cultural myths to advance
Chinese-American business / Charles Lee.
        p.   cm.
Includes index.
    ISBN 0-7931-6029-4 (6 × 9 pbk)
    1. Negotiation in business—China. 2. Negotiation in business—United States.
3. Business communication—China. 4. Business communication—United States.
5. Business communication—Cross-cultural studies. 6. Business etiquette—
China. 7. Corporate culture—China. 8. National characteristics, Chinese.
9. United States—Commerce—China. 10. China—Commerce—United States.
I. Title.
    HD58.6 .L44 2003
    658.4′052′0951—dc21

                                        2002015586

DEDICATION

To two ladies—Amy and Janet—who supported, advised, counseled, consoled, and generally suffered, through the painful birth of this book

CONTENTS

ACKNOWLEDGMENTS

Most of my adult life has been spent either working on management teams or helping to develop them. Not surprisingly then, when I set out to create this book, I first formed a team. My team members' names do not appear on the cover, although maybe they should, so I would like to acknowledge their contributions here. Everything that I am now telling you illustrates one of life's most important principles: You never know where a relationship will take you.

First of all, my dear friend and colleague Larry Servin gave me the inspiration for my book title: *Cowboys and Dragons*. Larry and his wife Susan also helped with the initial development of the book. Larry and Susan (who was my office temp in her college days) have adopted two young Chinese girls, and have already begun raising them as bicultural people. Larry's friendship with a woman in his church then led me to our literary agent, Jeanne Fredericks. Jeanne not only introduced me to our eventual book editor, Jean Iversen, but has proven to be a wonderfully skillful advisor regarding the book itself. Jean Iversen, in turn, introduced me to a very professional team at Dearborn Trade. Jeanne Fredericks also persuaded me early on that I needed a writer. I myself write in perfectly good "Chi-Merican."

Jeanne identified the person who has actually written the manuscript for *Cowboys and Dragons*, Dr. Peter Caldwell. I am one of those people who holds a lot of information inside, but needs help getting it out. So, Peter was able to ask the right questions to crack open the fortune cookie. Peter, in turn, knew of a Vermonter named Jeanne Wisner, who has actually been to China even more times than I have—over 150 separate trips guiding American tour groups. Jeanne has acted as our street savvy consultant on real life in China. (It almost sounds as though a conspiracy of Jeannes has been at work.)

On another thread of relationships, a long time ago I had a need for a public relations person to support a high-tech start-up firm, TranSwitch, that I helped found. At a venture capital luncheon, I met Elizabeth Howard, who has now agreed to help out as the publicist for *Cowboys and Dragons*. All of this has happened, I believe, not by *chance*, but by *design*— by what the Chinese call *guanxi*. At some level of our individual beings, we all intended to meet!

A number of other relationships have also threaded together into strands of *guanxi*. For instance, thanks to my wife Amy, we have moved from Connecticut to Florida, where one of our neighbors, Zima Zimmerman, recounted to me stories about Jewish people living in China, some for many centuries. Other neighbors have been willing readers of our rough manuscript, offering helpful hints to improve it, as did my son Alex.

Chinese *guanxi* goes back very far. I would like to take this opportunity to acknowledge the people who make up my longest and closest *guanxi* relationships—family, personal friendships, and business associates. First of all, my parents Johnny and Helen Lee; my wife Amy and children, Eric, Eric, and Alex; and my brother David and sisters Linda, Diana, Rosaline, and Clair have all contributed to my understanding of being first a "person" and then to my becoming a "bicultural person."

I have kept close relationships with a number of high school buddies and graduate school classmates: John Ho, Cyril Fu, and Dr. Alvin Tong I have known since school back in Taiwan. (Dr. Tong and I just ran a Triathlon together!) From the University of Minnesota, I have remained especially close to Dr. David Sippel, Dr. Gary Stroebel, and Dr. Jim Licari.

On the professional level, I would like to begin by acknowledging my Ph.D. dissertation advisor, Dr. Robert Plunkett, who trained me to develop fully my potential and to strive to continually improve myself, right up into the present. Arch McGill at AT&T not only gave me my first marketing job, he traveled to China with me in my first trip "home" in 1977 and selflessly encouraged me to become a "Chinese-American businessman." John Mahar of Exxon and Dr. Abe Zarem of Xerox taught me the ropes in venture capital investment and corporate development. Acer Chairman Stan Shih initially challenged me to write this book.

Former PRC Ambassador to the United States and United Nations, LI Dao Yu encouraged me to become a citizen of the world. Dr. Henry Kissinger enlarged my understanding of how diplomacy and business work together at a global level. Li Feng, a former VP at the Chinese MPT, gave me so many openings into telecommunications in China. Lastly, my close relations formed through venture capital have greatly enriched me personally and added to my understanding of international business: Jeff Ganek and Robert Poulin of NeuStar, Rick Montgomery of Mimix Broadband, Dr. Santanu Das of TranSwitch, and Origin Partners Managing Directors Scott Jones, Jim Hutchens, and Marc Yagjian.

A Thoroughly Bicultural Man

"Alex, your dad's like a Chinese fortune cookie—
so simple until you open him up."
—A FRIEND OF ALEX LEE'S, ABOUT CHARLES LEE

I woke up in a cold sweat, not knowing what country I was in. I had been standing in prison beside the men torturing my relatives. My relatives had done nothing wrong; their only "crime" was their blood tie to my father, who had been a minor official in CHIANG Kai-shek's Kuomintang ruling party before and during the Second World War. They cried out to me, but I could not reach them. In slow motion, living Technicolor horror, I saw it all and felt myself dragged down by guilt. Their hands stretched out toward me, and I could not help. Then I woke up.

Was I still in China's Beijing Hotel, or back home in New Jersey? For several long moments, I simply could not remember. I detected some familiar objects in my semidarkened bedroom. I merely faced another workday at AT&T headquarters.

The autumn of 1977 had come, and I had just returned from a business trip to mainland China—my first time there since my family had fled Shanghai for Taiwan in 1949. The terrible dreams had been going on every night since then for nearly two weeks, so I knew that I suffered from something more than jet lag. Some nights, I would dream of my relatives' torture or of searching for them and not being able to find them. Other nights, I would dream of walking through my successful life in America and becoming overwhelmed with guilt for not sharing my success with my poor Chinese relatives. Then the nightmares had turned to horrific scenes of blood and shrieking sheet metal as the expensive dream sports car I was driving crashed and burned. My life flashed in front of me—a crumpled waste. Whatever the nightmare, I would wake up disoriented. Can anyone tell me who I am?

Until the AT&T trip, I had not thought about China for a long time, at least since 1968, when I left the University of Minnesota for a career in corporate America. I had become thoroughly Americanized and shared the general ignorance of China's real situation as the Cultural Revolution ended. On my trip, I also learned that the Chinese did not understand America. They had talked a lot about American exploitation and about the Imperial Capitalists gaining at the expense of the rest of the world. Capitalist Pigs!

The nightmares affected my daily life as well. I had a job offer from Exxon, but I could not think clearly about it. Somehow, I had to stop the turmoil within me. Then one day I had a vision of Americans and Chinese actually getting to know one another and becoming friends! As a teenager on Taiwan, I had wanted to study diplomacy, but my father had forbidden it. Now, I vowed to become a man on a diplomatic mission: bringing prosperity to China through business ties with the United States. That night, I had my first sound sleep in two weeks. The nightmares left me and never returned.

THE MAKING OF A THOROUGHLY BICULTURAL MAN

I met with Arch McGill, the head of AT&T Marketing, who had approved my hiring and started the chain of events that had led to the Chinese mainland. When I told him that I was leaving AT&T, he was stunned. "Charles, how can you leave now! We've just gotten back from China!" At that time, AT&T was the biggest private company in the world—in everything but sales revenues; in revenues, Exxon was bigger. "Arch," I told him, "I'm going to work for a company even bigger than AT&T." "Charles, don't do it," he begged me. "Don't go and work for the government!"

Leaving AT&T was a tough choice given my newfound mission in life, but I felt that I could go nowhere there except up to the presidency of one of the 23 Bell operating companies. I had gone to AT&T to learn marketing but now felt it was time to move on. I wanted to get into new-venture formation, and I would join the new venture capital arm of the oil giant Exxon Enterprise. New ventures would somehow lead to China.

I had been catapulted my first day at AT&T from the bottom ranks of marketing management to a relationship with the man one step down from the chairmanship because Arch McGill was fascinated by Eastern civilization—and I was Chinese. Now at Exxon, I literally shot to the top of its corporate skyscraper in New York City my first week on the job! Why? The ruling Brahmins who ran the overall company had a Chinese delegation coming to visit them the following week and had no idea how to receive them. They found out somehow that I'd just been hired and called on me to plan the reception. Some years later, Exxon joined hands with the Communist Chinese to search together for Yellow Sea oil.

In addition to searching out new ventures for Exxon, and later Xerox, I began to study China for the first time—and America. I studied philosophy—Confucianism and Taoism for China; Socrates, Plato, Aristotle, and Alexander the Great for the West. It fascinated me that each civilization's thought and culture had developed and spread very widely, but independently of the other. My parents had been Buddhists; on Taiwan, my mother had converted to Christianity. I had become in practice an atheist. So I studied Buddhism and Christianity as well as the ancestor worship of traditional China. I worked at understanding the *why* that lay behind the specific *whats* for each civilization. I was becoming a thoroughly bicultural man.

My wife at the time, also a Chinese-American, had not wanted me to go to China, and she had refused to accompany me. She didn't want to open any doors closed within her. She also wanted her husband to be a nine-to-five, comfortable bureaucrat. Sadly, we parted. I was shedding my old skin and peeling away layers of my identity all at the same time.

ANGEL CAPITAL AND "THE PRINCELINGS"

I left the venture capital arm of Xerox Corporation in 1981 to found my own firm, called Lee and Satterlee, and to remarry. My new partner for life was not only thoroughly Chinese but an uncle of hers had been CHIANG Kai-shek's first premier. My business partner was thoroughly American, with a hint of oriental mystery about him: He never could learn how to sign his name the same way twice, so we constantly had trouble with traveler's checks that banks could not honor.

Satterlee and I entered the area of venture capital called seed money investing, identifying promising young start-ups too small to receive any major institutional financing and providing them with first-round cash in return for shares of company stock. The venture capital trade calls this money "angel capital."

While I learned how to run a business perceived as very high risk, other Chinese also took some risks of their own studying among the capitalists. The Chinese government sponsored a group of young visiting scholars, at such American schools as Harvard and Stanford, who were mainly sons and daughters of Communist Party leaders. Collectively, these young scholars were called "The Princelings" back home. When they later returned to China, they formed the nucleus of another risky venture—in Tiananmen Square (the Gate of Heavenly Peace).

One small group of Princelings, who studied business at Harvard and Stanford, became very interested in the relatively new venture capital industry America had spawned. They approached me in 1985 to help them help China, because I was the only Chinese-American running a venture capital firm at that time. By 1986, I had founded a new company called Abacus Ventures that would focus on telecom-related start-ups. My Chinese-American partner and I would look for ways that smaller companies could compete more effectively for new, international market opportunities, largely in the Pacific Rim. The Princelings and I made a good fit—working together for angel capital for China.

Together, we developed the proposal behind China's first venture capital fund—CVIC, or China Venturetech Investment Corporation—funded by the State Commission of Science and Technology. When Chinese Premier ZHAO Zi Yang approved the proposal, he told us, *"Cao cao de ban"*—literally "quiet quiet do it."

A BOOK GETS CONCEIVED

After CVIC, I became involved in a number of international business deals, often as a consultant helping Western and Eastern businesspeople understand one another and their very different ways of doing business. I learned that our differences—culturally derived—drive us apart in business and in life. We start with totally inaccurate preconceptions of each other, described in Part One of this book. Preconceptions, in turn, come from our very different histories, beliefs, and thought processes, described in Parts Two and Three. We also relate to one another very differently, as described in Part Four. Business opportunities exist in abundance, and each side possesses very good, although different, business skills. People problems, not business problems, destroy our mutual efforts, as I show you in Part Five. When I realized all of this, I began thinking about writing this book.

Then I happened to browse through a major book fair in Frankfurt, Germany, where I met a number of editors from American publishing houses. I told several of them about my idea for a book on Chinese-American business relations. "Charles," the man from Pegasus said, "there are so many books on China and America. What would make your book different?" "My book, once you'd read it, would allow you to be totally yourself with your Chinese counterparts and have a good relationship, and the same for the other side. Every other book tells you how to behave like the other side. That is very artificial and will never produce good relationships." Being real trumps artificiality every time.

DOING BUSINESS IN CHINA

The question that every other business book on China tries to answer— *How* do I do business in China?—is the wrong question in the first place! How can you get a right answer when you start with the wrong question? *How* I can do business in China can only be effectively addressed after I first answer the three Ws—*who, why,* and *what*. Who are the Chinese, and who am I as an American? Why does the other side behave as it does, and why do we behave as we do? What does the other side want, and what is it that we want? Only when we know each other can we ask how we can do business together.

Notice what happens when we follow the three Ws: We first share knowledge about ourselves and who we are and then why we behave as we do. Consider greeting rituals: Americans learn from early childhood to greet people with a firm handshake; Chinese have been taught to bow. If I shake hands with my Chinese counterparts, I find that they shake hands very weakly. Ah ha! I think. They are wimps! In reality, they have not learned how to shake hands like Americans because they don't know *why* we shake hands as we do. If I bow, as the "how-to" books tell us, the Chinese think, how condescending.

If I also explain to my Chinese counterpart when I shake hands why it is that Americans shake hands so firmly, then he or she understands something important about me: A firm handshake shows confidence and interest in the other party. If we bow and I inquire why the Chinese do this, I learn a great deal about respect for the other person's role and about a high regard for harmony. Shake *and* bow—and know why you're doing it.

Once we have shared knowledge about ourselves openly, learning why we behave as we do, we can then accept the other party as they are and who they are. We can then become friends. Understanding and friendship, in turn, allow us to discuss openly our respective interests and jointly to develop a mutually beneficial plan of action. Cooperation replaces narrow self-interest. When people cease to be the problem, business problems get solved relatively easily.

THE THREE Ws FOR EAST-WEST BUSINESS SUCCESS

Before you even think of asking *how* to do business in China (or the East generally), first learn the answers to these questions:

- *Who* is the other party from a cultural perspective, and *who* are we?
- *Why* does the other party behave as it does, and *why* do we?
- *What* does the other party want from us, and vice versa?

The people model for success: Knowledge about *who, why,* and *what* leads to acceptance, leads to friendship, leads to successful shared business actions.

PART ONE

Preconceptions and Reality

Question: How can I do business in China?
Answer: You do not know enough yet to understand the answer to your own
question. (A very Chinese way of regarding questions about China)

A close friend of mine inadvertently provided my book title. "Charles," he asked me, "what one symbol best characterizes American businessmen in the eyes of their Chinese counterparts, and vice versa?" Without even thinking, I shot back, "Cowboys and Dragons."

Origin of the Word Cowboy: *Banditi.* Name applied to lawless villains operating from behind British lines during the American Revolution.

Americans regard cowboys as good guys, forgetting that they can also be bandits and cattle rustlers. The Chinese perceive American Cowboy behavior in both these senses but more in the second, particularly because Americans participated in the 19th-century exploitation of their country. The Cowboys are all looters, the Dragons think.

The same cultural confusion arises over the Dragon symbol. In Western tradition originating with the ancient Greeks, the beast is a mythic,

1

A Chinese Definition for Dragon: The Dragon is a benevolent beast made up of the best parts of nine different animals. Dragon bodies are covered with nine times nine scales—an extreme of a lucky number. Dragons come in four sorts: Celestial, Spiritual, Earth, and Treasure. Only Celestial Dragons possess five toes on their feet; the rest have but three or four.

scaly reptile that guards treasure hoards; slay the dragon and get the gold. The British tried to do just that in the 19th-century Opium Wars.

For the Chinese, the Dragon possesses mythical properties and can ascend and descend from Heaven to the nether regions of earth. Because a dragon brought the first emperor down from Heaven to the Middle Kingdom, it became the national symbol and the badge of the imperial family. The Chinese see themselves as either sons or daughters of the Dragon. Does the Dragon block the way to riches or guard the treasure hoard against invaders?

Both the Cowboy *and* the Dragon assume mythical proportions. Like the Dragon, the Cowboy is larger than life and occupies all space between Heaven and the nether regions.

Part One begins by revealing and disarming a number of each side's preconceptions about the other—all in terms of Cowboy and Dragon motifs. Only then can the finger-pointing stop: "*You* are all greedy," say the Dragons. "*You* are shifty and sneaky," respond the Cowboys. In reality, neither preconception happens to be true.

DRAGONS COME IN FOUR SORTS

1. *Celestial Dragons (tian-long).* These Dragons guard the Heavens and protect the mansions of the gods. A "poh shan" appears on the tops of their heads, which enables them to ascend and descend from heaven to earth.

2. *Spiritual Dragons (shen-long).* As Weather Lords, these Dragons can be very combative; when Weather Lords fight, they cause whirl-

winds, waterspouts, and other such natural catastrophes. It is best to avoid offending them.

3. *Earth Dragons (di-long).* These Dragons hide in ponds, rivers, lakes, and seas. They rule the waters, and their battles cause mighty storms. Best stay on their good side, too.

4. *Treasure Dragons (fun-can-long).* These Dragons have charge of all the precious minerals buried in the ground. Each has a magical dragon pearl hanging from its chin. Tickle a Treasure Dragon's chin, and dragon pearls will reproduce themselves for you. Of course, getting close to a Treasure Dragon can be a ticklish business in itself!

CHAPTER ONE

Cowboys and Dragons

INTERGALACTIC TRAVEL

Imagine that two groups of people meet, each from a different world. One group travels from planet Athenea to meet people who live on Zhong, a voyage Starship Enterprise might make. They travel as peaceful merchants rather than as warriors or government officials—"citizen diplomats." Merchants and businesspeople pioneer foreign relations, being closest to real human needs and desires and most desirous of seeking out new opportunities. Trade births understanding.

We would expect the same situation as when foreigners meet on planet Earth: Language differences immediately breed confused communications. The two groups may speak different "silent languages" as well—such as those of personal space and relative time, and even of food. Different systems of agreements and of law and property further muddy the seemingly simple matter of who wants to sell and to buy what. In a joint venture, goals and profit reckoning will conflict. The relative value of each side's contribution—be it labor, capital, or technology—will also cause disputes. Progress resembles a rocky road.

Let us write the script this way: The Planet Zhong people have learned that Planet Athenea possesses a remarkable advanced technology for making a strong, lightweight, highly resilient textile material that can be used both for personal apparel and for certain applications in the aerospace industry. The Planet Zhong businesspeople want above all access to this new technology. The Planet Athenea businesspeople have come on a trade mission to sell millions of meters of the material, while keeping the technology secret. Planet Athenea, however, does not have enough inexpensive labor available to run the machinery making those millions of meters. One side wants cheap labor and new markets, the other access to technology. The trade mission hits a speed bump.

Eventually, the two groups may resolve upon a joint manufacturing scheme where a Planet Athenea business contributes the technology and capital for a Planet Zhong factory to supply both planets with the material. Planet Athenea may also agree to license the technology to Planet Zhong after so many years, for a large fee. After all, if trade breeds understanding, eventually the Planet Zhong businesspeople will figure out the technology anyhow. Just as likely, the two groups will spend months, or even years, talking past one another and fail to reach any agreement at all. Everyone ends up poorer.

Sneak preview for a coming Star Wars Intergalactic Commerce series? Hardly. Planet Athenea is the United States and Planet Zhong is China. The story takes place some years after World War II. The high-technology product? Nylon. If the time frame were shifted back 2,000 years, the product might well have been silk—the first miracle thread. Contact between China and Rome would have been made over the old Silk Road. China, after all, was the first high-tech nation, the first America.

The Internet is the New Silk Road, and America is the New China.

AMERICANS ARE COWBOYS; CHINESE ARE DRAGONS

Even though both Americans and Chinese do in fact dwell on a single Earth, we might as well inhabit two different planets. We are simply that different, even though we are both species Homo sapiens—wise men. Look at Dr. John Gray's best-seller *Men Are from Mars; Women Are from Venus*, which argues that men and women behave so differently that they might as well come from different planets. Mars and Venus convey this sense of seemingly other-planetary origins that exist even between intimate lovers. The same holds for West and East. We look and behave like extraterrestrials to each other.

What two very different lands might the Americans and Chinese come from? The popular imagination in each country suggests the images of the Cowboy and the Dragon. For the Chinese people, all Americans come from the badlands populated by Cowboys. For Americans, the Chinese inhabit the mysterious lands of the Dragons. We each "communicate . . . , think, feel, perceive, react, respond, love, need, and appreciate differently." Dr. Gray got it right for East-West relations, too.

For instance, Americans think in terms of private and public spaces for living. They value private property highly: Don't touch my stuff! In China until recently, everything belonged to the emperor. The Chinese don't have an equivalent word for *privacy*. Even the toilets are open and public!

> For Cowboys, personal space exists in the external world; for Dragons, personal space is internal. In China, it is not rude to move aside a person who is blocking your way: All space is public.

For the Chinese, the symbol for America is the Marlboro Man! Large, tough, weathered, the Marlboro cowboy always rides tall in the saddle, looking far into the distance, and he always ride alone. No families and ancestors exist in his world; he has no roots. Marlboro men always move onward, pushing into some new frontier—western lands, science, space. They do wild and dangerous things with total abandon and freedom, but they show no respect for the past. They seem to have no past, or any need of one. They are loners.

To Americans, the land of the Dragons has long, snaky, green beasts populating it, seemingly with thousands of legs and smoke blowing out of their nostrils. Underneath each dragon costume, hundreds of little people with no identities make the beasts move. They engage in thousand-year-old rituals each New Year's Day, but they are poor and backward. They work incredibly hard but produce relatively little, because they lack modern tools. They also lack individual identities. They appear benign but may be dangerous in their very numbers. After all, the West traditionally feared Dragons and marked treacherous places on maps with this warning: "There be Dragons here!"

> Cowboys are men; Dragons are women.

Of course, each of these images appears laughable—to the other culture's people. And they would be benign, except that they cause us to prejudge others. We enter into a business relationship and immediately perceive that "they" are just what we thought all along. It is as though we have been told that so-and-so is a braggart. Then we meet so-and-so and hear him speak excitedly about his new car. We say to ourselves, "See, he *is* a braggart," and thus utterly miss his boyish enthusiasm and charm. Our own preconceptions prevent us from detecting such things as the creativity and inventiveness of the Chinese or the compassion and generosity of the Americans. The images of the Cowboy and Dragon reveal how utterly strange our lands are to each other. Where do these differences come from?

STRANGE LANDS

Eastern and Western civilizations developed almost totally independently from their inceptions until only about a millennium ago. The first contacts between East and West did not begin until about 250 B.C. with the establishment of the Silk Road. This intercourse came too late to affect the evolving institutions of either land. Over perhaps 5,000 years, each land evolved complex arrays of social arrangements—such as spoken language, writing, property rules, and work practices. Different environments assured different results—even from identical human needs.

For instance, the Chinese heartland has little building stone, so Chinese architecture developed a style in sympathy with nature: buildings of wood. Structure encouraged harmony, and Chinese art emphasized harmony with nature by merging a painting's background into the surrounding environment. To this day, Chinese art does not get framed. Because harmony discouraged abrupt change, the Chinese language did not develop verb tenses. Experience determines language.

In the West, stone building materials encouraged monument architecture and the cult of the "great man." Western art set off a painting from the surrounding world to emphasize its individuality, its creative uniqueness. Portrait painting began early in the West but never developed in the East. A succession of failed, violent rulers yielded a sense of continual change and flux; language took on past, present, and future tenses for action. Over time, the graveyards filled with indispensable leaders.

When American architect Frank Lloyd Wright (1867–1959) wanted to break from a restrictive form framed by classical architecture, not surprisingly he looked to the East for a model. The Prairie Style resulted, a fusion of Eastern harmony and Western naturalism. Form finally found harmony with its setting. East and West shook hands.

China has stood as the representative Eastern civilization for almost 5,000 years. During the 20th century, the United States has emerged as the leading Western civilization. As America and China become more and more intertwined, will we get to know each other for better or for worse? The future of the whole world depends on how well we relate. And that in turn depends on whether people from two very different lands can really understand one another. Can Mars talk to Venus?

WHY WE DIFFER

Here we must be very careful. We will not become alike. Our differences will remain, because they have had 5,000 years to grow. We need to better understand *why* we have such pervasive, everyday differences—not just in *what* regard we differ *how*. Why trumps every other card in the East-West deck.

Consider, for instance, how Cowboys and Dragons use numbers in everyday transactions. A Cowboy will say, "I'll give you 30 percent off the normal purchase price." His Dragon counterpart will say instead, "I will only charge you 70 percent of the whole price." Or consider how the two make change. A Cowboy will count out change by stating the purchase price and counting upward to the whole amount received, beginning with the smallest denomination of change and working up to the largest. A dragon, on the other hand, will say, "Here is your change for . . . ," and then state the whole amount given. Then he or she will count out the change beginning with the largest denomination and working down to the smallest. Big deal, or small deal?

In business, counting is a big deal. Cowboys and Dragons count in different units. Cowboys use hundred, thousand, hundred thousand, million, and billion. Dragons use Chinese words for hundred, thousand, "ten thousand," and "one hundred million." This causes huge arguments over project budgets. Where Cowboys say million, Dragons say "one-hundred ten thousands." Neither side understands the other! Missing by one zero, of course, can have huge consequences. Translate carefully!

For a Dragon, the concept of the whole has great importance. So a Dragon always offers a special price as a part of a whole and begins making change with the round sum. The significance of these simple social arrangements lies in the inner thinking related to them. Making change represents only a minor example of a fundamental difference—a pebble in the pond making its first tiny ring in the water.

Westerners think fractionally, whereas Easterners think holistically.

Look what happens as the pattern of rings spreads; Americans like to break things down into their bits and pieces. "Thirty percent off" is a breaking-down activity: fractionating. They like to analyze things and then put them back together. Americans have always been fascinated by how things work and how to make them work better. They believe, however, that anything has only so many discrete parts—something that derives from materialistic science. The Chinese believe that hierarchies of concepts and ideas have no limit—all of them forming a whole. Like an infinite number of Russian Matroushka doll pieces, concepts may be unboxed or all put back one inside the other. Our history determines how we think.

How I Learned about the Whole and Its Parts

I learned this when I was in junior high school on Taiwan. I had begun to feel that I was a failure because I couldn't become number one in my class in any single discipline. I was always number two. Then a friend told me, "Charles, you are better than any of them!" "How can that be so?" I asked. "I am first in nothing." He answered, "If you must compare yourself to others, compare the *whole* of you to the *whole* of them." That was the dawn of my realization that life needs to be looked at as a totality, which is, in truth, very Chinese.

Later, I learned that the West sees the individual as more important than the family or a work group, or the nation for that matter. The smallest part is bigger than the whole. The Chinese see that as a harmful fractionating of the whole. How the harmony of the whole may become disrupted by the individual concerns the Chinese far more than how the individual pieces function or the freedom of the individual. Because the whole is so important, the Chinese hesitate to disrupt it unless the need grows very great. This explains why "face" has such importance. The conduct of a leader represents the whole group and cannot safely be individuated. Americans, on the other hand, see the individual as the source of all action. Thus, the individual receives scrutiny and gets judged publicly, over even the minutest details of conduct. The whole can take care of itself.

In this regard, the Chinese find the 2000 American presidential election very upsetting—representing the boundless pursuit of individual gain over the welfare of the whole nation. A number of my Chinese friends have recently told me, "See, Charles, I told you that the one-party system is better!"

THE ART OF THE DEAL, EAST AND WEST

Now look what often happens when East and West meet in a business deal. Chinese and American businesspeople come together to form a joint venture, and both sides agree to "make money"! They remain elated for a short time, and then the questions get asked that start an argument: "How much money?" "How soon?" The Americans answer "as much as possible as soon as possible." The Chinese reply "some" and "over the long term." The two sides disagree violently without ever knowing why. The Chinese don't know that American thinking gets driven by corporate shareholder demands and quarterly profit statements. They also don't realize that for Americans a job is a means to other ends: to living well personally. A successful business deal means a big bonus. Big deal, big bonus.

The Americans who work to live don't know that the Chinese live for work, that their work group or unit makes up a daily surrogate family for their lifetimes. The Chinese worry about long-term employment for everyone in their work group and personal families—even the nation— far more than making a lot of money quickly. The American behavior stems from the demands of the marketplace; Chinese behavior goes back to the idea that the Emperor takes care of everybody—and that gets accomplished only when everyone in the social hierarchy cares for those below him or her. As a result, Americans can engage in isolated profit analysis and reach decisions quickly; the Chinese must take a longer time to decide because they must reach a holistic consensus that considers a business deal's impact on everyone. Big deal, many mouths to feed. Who's greater good gets pursued?

Chief Cowboy now looks Chairman Dragon dead in the eye. All of the Cowboy's training tells him: Make strong eye contact, show great interest, be earnest—and close the deal! His Dragon counterpart responds by looking modestly aside. His training tells him: Show respect to the foreigners by avoiding direct eye contact. Don't look too eager; if you hold out, you may get a better deal. One stares; the other looks away. They never even look at one another! The deal goes south.

HOW TO REALLY PUT YOUR FOOT IN IT

Without understanding how the other side thinks, both Cowboys and Dragons will inevitably judge their opposite numbers badly. We often find that we have offended and angered the other party without ever meaning to. For example, an American businessman may wish to pay his Chinese counterpart a compliment. They have, after all, begun to form a good relationship. So he says, "Mr. Chen, you look so young!" In America, of course, that is a great compliment to a senior executive who has begun to show his years—a little bit of a white lie but a great compliment. Imagine the American's reaction when Mr. Chen becomes flustered and angry, and pulls back from the budding relationship.

Why? What has gone wrong? In China, people generally value tradition and the wisdom that comes with age. The boss *should* appear older than his subordinates; that way, they will respect him. So Mr. Chen believes that the rude American has just challenged his competence and judgment! What should the American have said to compliment Mr. Chen? "Mr. Chen, you are *so* energetic!" That will please him immensely—and it may even be true.

I ASK MY DIRECTOR FOR A DATE

Be careful, too, about light banter, which the Chinese don't understand. Chinese doesn't even have a word for what Americans call *humor.* When I first arrived at the University of Minnesota, I reported to the Foreign Student Office and said, "I am Charles Lee, and I am here to make a date with the director." The secretary laughed and said, "Mr. Lee, you mean an appointment!" I couldn't see the humor in my confusing the two words. Of course, I did not want an intimate meeting with a female senior faculty member! I became very serious and insisted that I wanted a date—and I felt shamed by her laughter. Now, of course, I can laugh at such things and at myself. This is very American.

OUR DIFFERING HUMAN LANDSCAPES

- *Eye contact.* For Cowboys, making eye contact with another conveys sincerity and personal interest. Look 'em dead in the eye when you speak. The Chinese have been taught never to look directly at any-

one, because that shows a lack of deference and proper decorum—
except among lovers! In the old days, if you stared into the eyes of
the Emperor, you lost your head. In America, when a parent disciplines a child, she tells the child, "Shame on you! Look at me!" In
China, when a father disciplines his son, he will say, "Shame on you!
Don't you dare look up at me!" Do you see how early on Cowboys
and Dragons learn totally different social behaviors?

- *Learning.* Beginning in the earliest grades, Americans are taught to
  behave as individuals in school, questioning and even challenging
  their teachers. Questions allow teachers to know how bright you are.
  In China, everybody listens quietly and takes notes—no questioning, even in graduate school. Questioning would be an improper
  challenge to the teacher's authority. Test results tell teachers how
  bright you are. These traditions go back to Socrates on the one hand,
  who asked why, and to Confucius on the other hand, who said,
  "There is no why. That's how it is."

- *Authority.* Cowboys and Dragons have very different ways of showing respect to superiors. In China, the boss walks in front of his subordinates. In a meeting, the Chinese leader of a group always speaks,
  even if a recognized Chinese expert in the subject happens to be
  present. If the leader is not present, the number two person speaks.
  Deference moves downward. The boss always sits in the middle of
  group members—to show harmony. In America, the boss delegates.
  Americans engage in shared speaking by successive professional experts. You please your boss by performing well in a meeting.

- *Humor.* There is no Chinese root word for *humor* as social give and
  take because everything has always been taken seriously, with deference to the order of things. It would never do to tell a joke about a
  friend or relative; that would undermine face. Humor as we Americans know it is a challenge to the social order, something we do will-
  ingly in America but something the Chinese don't even understand.
  That is not to say by any means that the Chinese are humorless and
  therefore dull people. Jokes and even comic theater certainly exist,
  and Chinese people laugh a lot together. There is, however, a boundary between a funny story and individual face. A Chinese person
  may even say "I am going to tell a joke" before telling it, so that
  everyone listening understands that the speaker has moved across
  the boundary into humor. When I first lived in America, I had to
  study American humor very seriously in order to understand it.
  Now, after a long time, I find many American jokes very funny.

- *Debate.* Cowboys love to debate issues and may become direct and even personal in supporting their positions. When the debate is over, they can shake hands and go back to being friendly. Good form among Cowboys requires that the individual not take things said in debate personally. Dragons find this behavior quite horrifying and very dishonest. In China, you never speak in a way that could cause a friend to lose face, a tradition with ancient roots, symbolized by the realities of language: Western language is conceptual whereas Chinese language is imagistic. Dragons do not separate the concept from the person the way we do in the West.
- *Competition.* Cowboys love rodeos, where each individual competes directly against all others. In the tradition of the American West, the quickest draw gains immense respect. Dragons avoid this sort of direct competition because it threatens social harmony. That doesn't mean the Chinese don't compete vigorously for gain—but the gain takes a social, not an individual, form.
- *Sexual innuendo.* Sexual fulfillment, of course, forms a very basic need along with food within both the East and West, but they are expressed very differently. Dragons talk ceaselessly in public about food—but never about sex. That is for intimate lovers and the family only. Americans have sexualized romantic love in a manner that makes public displays of affection normative.

RECOMMENDATIONS

1. *Eye contact.* Find an opportunity to explain to your Chinese counterpart why Americans seek to make direct eye contact. Then you become free to be yourself, without offending the other party. Before you explain, avoid making strong eye contact.
2. *Reasons for actions.* Don't push your Chinese counterparts for the rational explanations behind their decisions. You won't get an answer, or you'll get an answer to a question you never asked at all!
3. *Presentations.* Explain up front why you allow more than one member of your group to speak and why your group's members may even disagree in public. Otherwise, the Chinese will ask among themselves, "Who is in charge on the American side?"
4. *Humor and sexual innuendo.* Don't even try them until you know your Chinese counterparts well enough to explain what Americans use them for.

5. *Competition.* Americans use competition between teams to stimulate progress; the Chinese don't. Always talk about and encourage progress in terms of mutual cooperation. Never challenge the Chinese to a competition.

6. *Language.* Chinese is not a language from which you adopt a few words to impress the natives. A Chinese word inserted into an English sentence will not even be recognized as Chinese by a Dragon. *Do* consider learning a few short Chinese sentences to show respect. *Don't* try to speak Chinese or use a smattering of Chinese words to impress your counterparts. If you don't *really* know Chinese, your efforts will seem patronizing and will fail.

7. *Culture and civilization.* Each side needs to learn respect for the other's long history of culture and civilization. Explain the background of what you say and do from a cultural inheritance point of view; and listen to the other party from the same point of view. Then members of each party can be totally themselves and be accepted by the other side.

CHAPTER TWO

How Dragons View Cowboys

FLATLANDERS

The Four Legs of the Culture Beast: Cultural awareness has four dimensions as does the space-time continuum: historical/traditional, social/pop-cultural, political, and economic.

How many dimensions do we see when we look at the people of another culture or of our own? Americans often equate the term *culture* with current pop culture; Cowboys look at other cultures through the same pop culture lenses. Within culture, Americans may include a social dimension, often defined by the insights of TV sitcoms. Cowboys easily forget other dimensions, such as history, political arrangements, and economic structures. They see a world that is totally flat. To imagine what gets missed, consider what it would be like to live in a world of only two dimensions—or, even worse, a world of only one, like a string!

Edwin Abbot's classic book *Flatland* describes life for a bunch of people stuck in 2-D. They have no sense of depth. If you want to feel uncomfortable, read it.

DRAGONS HAVE 3-D VISION

Dragons, with their 3-D vision, don't picture American culture as a flatland. Their cultural perspective of America possesses more topographical detail. Of course, the topography of one culture emerges only when contrasted with another. The Chinese compare American culture to their own—with frequently interesting results. From the peaks of Chinese history, they particularly focus on just three aspects of overall American culture: *wealth, power,* and *creativity.* Which end of the telescope do they look into?

> Cowboys see a pop cultural flatland; dragons view the cultural landscape from the 5,000-year-old peaks of Eastern history.

Love Me Tender: A Chinese Pop Cultural Look at Cowboys and American Wealth

The Chinese image of American wealth amuses Cowboys the most: Americans play around all day. They consume vast quantities of energy, but they don't work hard as the Chinese do. They enjoy themselves. They loiter around and sing to one another. They are like—Elvis Presley!

> *Western Wasteland:* Wasteful consumption bothers the Chinese, who see the California energy crisis not as a supply or market failure but as the way that nature punishes careless people who have no concern for the greater good.

Elvis still fascinates older Chinese; younger Chinese prefer Madonna and Michael Jackson. The Chinese do not, however, regard cultural icons in the same manner that Americans do. The older Chinese see Elvis as a symbol of American degeneracy. Elvis represents forbidden behavior. For the younger generation, Madonna stands for freedom.

The older Chinese perceive something socially adolescent about Americans, who like to behave as though they are forever young and in hot pursuit of the opposite sex. They don't care for family and traditional relationships. And these adolescent Americans can be so touchy about their personal "rights"—don't you dare step on my shoes. They make

inordinate demands upon others—"love me tender, love me true"—
without offering anything in return.

The Chinese feel more than a little jealous of American wealth and
active leisure, just as they are repulsed by the expressions the wealth and
leisure frequently take. Of course, this seems amusing to Americans, who
in reality work very hard. Nevertheless, truth is a dog that can bite.

Pax Americana

The Chinese both admire and distrust American power, just as they do
its wealth. They feel uneasy about how Americans will use their power—
whether to maintain world peace or to expropriate the wealth of others.
They also want to know more about the sources of American ascendancy.
How did these "foreign devils" overcome the power of the Dragon?

Distrust of American power stems from two sources: (1) past American military actions and missionary zeal in China and (2) American
"preachiness." Few Americans even know that their country participated
in a direct invasion and occupation of coastal China during the 19th century. Consequently, Cowboys have little understanding of Dragon sensi-
tivities when being lectured about "human rights" and other Chinese
internal policies. Nobody likes being lectured to.

For instance, when American historians and diplomats talk about the
"loss of China" after World War II, that can really offend Dragons. The
Chinese regard the "communist takeover" as the reestablishment of
China's rights within its own territory. Similarly, the British look on the
turning over of Hong Kong with nostalgia for their colonial past; Dragons
see it as Hong Kong's "return to the Motherland."

Generally speaking, the Chinese have come to resent what they see as
the American tendency toward moralistic harangues combined with
immoral conduct. Dragons quickly seize on America's poor record of race
relations as proof of Cowboy hypocrisy; and they also know something
about the hypocrisy surrounding fallen American TV evangelists. Be
careful to whom you preach.

As for the sources of American political and economic power, the Chinese look at Americans' ability to organize systematically for any action,
American technological prowess, and Cowboys' pistols. None of these
sources resembles the Dragon power the Chinese ascribe to themselves,
which they traditionally believe descends to them from an all-powerful
heaven through mythical dragons to national, clan, and family hierarchies. Who knows where these alien Cowboys come from?

They particularly distrust the armed Cowboys who appear driven by "greed": American *lawyers!* These modern Cowboys use words and legal agreements as weapons for carrying out theft. The Chinese prefer to deal with American engineers and research scientists—the real creators of American wealth and power. Keep the armed bandits away!

> Dragons typically show up at a meeting with lots of engineers; Cowboys come with sales/marketing guys and hired guns—their lawyers.

Cowboy Creativity

Cowboy creativity has changed the world forever. The Chinese perceive the American spirit as innovative, venturesome, and highly individualistic. The Cowboy appears both as the loner with no overriding social attachments and as a rugged and courageous figure, one who builds up the frontier and uses pistols to defend personal honor and the honor of others. He is the creative force in a vast and empty landscape. He is also the hired gun, occupying a landscape where the fastest draw wins. The Chinese, too, have cowboys in their thinly populated interior, but they don't have the American Cowboy's heroic and threatening dual nature. Hero or villain?

> The Cowboy who is the fastest draw wins; the Dragon who stands out above the others gets hammered down.

The Chinese myth of the American Cowboy includes the figure of the Marlboro Man, as well as the vivid imagery of Remington's rodeo cowboy sculpture. The myth applies to the American fighter pilots of World War II and the Korean conflict and to the American athlete. The Chinese admire American athletic prowess but not our athletes' brash behavior. To the Chinese, American athletes of all ages behave like adolescents.

The Cowboy also stands for the American entrepreneur—the individual who joins together American innovation, efficiency, and wealth generation. Here, all three basic Chinese perceptions of Americans come together: wealth, power, and creativity. The Chinese admire Bill Gates and Michael Jordan—and now Tiger Woods.

REBELS WITH A CAUSE

The Chinese perceive two things about American Cowboys: They are all very young and rebellious. They are all like Elvis. The Dragons see these traits so readily because the Chinese view America through cultural lenses darkened by hardship that cause them to see with a respect for elders, tradition, and authority. Age and youth; darkness and light.

The Cowboy heroes of Silicon Valley are rebels with a cause; the cause: to transform the world through advanced technology. They don't fear trying something that has never been done before. Dragons look on such creativity as dangerous rebelliousness—a threat to the entire social order. In this manner, Silicon Valley Cowboys also generate a lot of Dragon envy.

> Dragons see reality through dark lenses; Cowboys always wear rose-colored glasses.

What Dragons don't see about the youthful Cowboy entrepreneurs of America is how often they fail—and how they handle failure. Michael Dell stands out as an exception—one of a very few who has not failed. Look how often Bill Gates failed before he made Microsoft into an international triumph. When a young Cowboy high-tech entrepreneur fails, he simply takes it as a lesson in life and sets out to get his venture right the next time. Young Cowboys actively seek risky ventures for the thrill of it.

> Dragons think that Cowboys are technologically clever *children*; frequently missing the strenuous labor and solid technological grounding that underlie the adolescent behavior.

Dragons, on the other hand, cannot conceive of such risky behavior, because failure, with its loss of face, carries a high price in China. In fact, failure becomes doubly punishing in China, where it also reflects badly on a person's work unit or other group. In comparison, individual failure in America has little social stigma attached to it. So Cowboys venture boldly where Dragons fear to tread.

East Meets West at XDC

Consider the founder of Apple. When I worked for Xerox Development Corporation (XDC) in the late 1970s, I had the pleasure of meeting a very youthful Stephen Jobs, who presented his business plan to us. He had dropped out of college to roam around Asia for some time "finding himself" within the ancient East—a traditional adolescent American luxury. In Asia, he learned firsthand how badly Asian peasants needed small, inexpensive tools, which started him thinking how badly Americans needed a small, inexpensive personal computer as a tool. I recommended and received approval for a $1 million second-round financing deal for fledgling Apple Computer. We both understood and applied the tool analogy. Our thinking in this regard was very Chinese.

DRAGON MISPERCEPTIONS OF COWBOYS

Cowboys seeking business opportunities in China will likely encounter the following four basic misperceptions about America to which they need satisfactory responses.

1. America has no traditions to give it strength and continuity.
2. America has terrible racial problems and a repressive past.
3. America's political system is a rash and new experiment that is likely to fail.
4. Consumerism is a wasteful new idea that Americans have just recently developed.

In the following sections, I suggest some reasonable responses that the Chinese with their long view of history will understand.

Notice that these perceptions match the four general areas of cultural awareness with which the chapter began: historical/traditional, social, political, and economic. Each perception turns out to be untrue—or at best a partial truth. Cowboys must understand and convey the real truths about these misperceptions.

Cowboys Have No History

To begin with, Dragons need to perceive America as the continuation of a Western culture with roots nearly as old as China's. Not only that,

America has drawn into it many people from the East, so that it contains aspects of Eastern culture as well. America has become the space where West and East can meet together in peace. Be prepared to recount some positive legends of the Western world, such as Socrates' life.

They Are All Racists

Yes, America has had terrible racial problems, but Dragons miss the reality of America's long historic effort to achieve a nondiscriminatory society. It is a little ironic that Dragons know about America's conflicted racial past, but still think that America has no history: Perceptions are not always internally consistent. Dragons seldom know that America fought a terrible civil war on behalf of the rights of all Americans—and that includes Chinese-Americans, too. Who will inform them, if you don't?

America Is a Rash Experiment That Will Fail

Sadly, few Cowboys realize that the American political system has deep roots in a more than 2,000-year-old Western tradition. These roots reach downward in good soil to the ancient Greeks and early Romans. The tree of liberty has also been nourished by the Renaissance and Enlightenment thinkers of Italy, France, and Great Britain. More immediately, American democracy sprang from the 17th-century writings of the Englishman John Locke. Americans fail to tell the Chinese about their past because they know it so imperfectly themselves. Cowboys like to live only for the future. But you can change that.

They Are All So Wasteful

Last, consumerism was not invented in America but rather in western Europe, where market institutions replaced older forms of social control. It is hard for Dragons to balance the advantages of market efficiencies with the looser forms of social control that markets provide Americans. Cowboys can point out that Americans work very hard, just as the Chinese do, and that Americans' hard work is motivated by the discipline stemming from a market economy. Nothing so concentrates a Cowboy's efforts as having bills to pay.

THE MOSQUITO EFFECT

Actually, consumerism has even reached China. China now has as many as *300 million* former peasants who have left the land to seek better lives in the thriving cities. And in those cities, many of the same ills have developed as we experience in America. A Cowboy may carefully and indirectly refer to the reality that market economies bring good and bad changes in both America *and* China. By the way, the Chinese cope with these new changes by adopting a figurative bit of speech they call *the mosquito effect*: "When the doors are opened, the gnats and mosquitoes come in as well as the people."

> The word *peasant* has become politically incorrect. The Chinese call members of this social class *farmers*.

A LOVE-HATE RELATIONSHIP

The sky is high, and the Emperor is far away.
—AN OLD CHINESE PROVERB

The Dragon view of Cowboy life and behavior can be summed up as what may be fairly described as a love-hate relationship stemming from long memory. Dragons easily recall the many centuries of China's own technological superiority over the West that really ended only with the Industrial Revolution. So Dragons admire American advanced technology and wealth, but they bitterly resent the naïve assumption that America has been the first nation on earth to attain supremacy in either. Dragons like to picture Europeans living nasty, brutish lives in caves when their own ancestors enjoyed civilized opulence. They react even more strongly to present-day Americans: They are *so* arrogant!

> Dragons possess a memory like an elephant's. Cowboys say, "Forget it."

Dragons make one of two responses to what they see as an American arrogance of power and wealth, neither particularly flattering. The young educated Dragons see Cowboy arrogance and wish to emulate it. The older educated ones resent American supremacy, feeling that it is not deserved. They also resent the American belief that the Chinese live in communist bondage. Dragons admire American freedom, but they think that they are even *freer* than the Cowboys! After all, Cowboy freedom is limited by laws. In China, so long as you avoid the attention of a remote government official, you can engage in whatever business practices you wish to. You can do anything you want: *The sky is high, and the Emperor is far away*!

CERTAIN DRAGON PERCEPTIONS OF COWBOYS

- *Cowboys shoot from the hip.* They draw quick conclusions and take rash actions.
- *Cowboys are like technologically clever children.* They play around all day on computers but lack cultural roots and depth.
- *They are impatient.* Hold out, and you can always get a better deal.
- *They are interested only in personal gain.* Watch out for their lawyers, who only want to steal from you.
- *They are part of a 100-year-old history of theft and unfair dealing.* Their ancestors forced China to accept very unfair agreements at the point of a gun.
- *They are so arrogant!*

RECOMMENDATIONS

1. *Check your pistols at the door.* When dealing with Dragons, leave the lawyers behind until you reach a basic oral understanding with your Chinese counterparts.
2. Learn some basic Western, as well as some Chinese, history (see the bibliography for a few suggestions). What you don't know can blindside you during subtle negotiations. To the Chinese, history is not bunk; it is an ever-present reality.
3. *Do not* always lead with your sales/marketing people. The Chinese want to talk to, and learn from, your technical people.

4. *Do* leave your soapbox at home. The Chinese didn't ask you to deliver a sermon from Mount Rushmore!

5. *Do* find the opportunity to explain that American heritage carries on a Western civilization that dates back to the ancient Greeks and the Roman Empire.

A COWBOY AND A DRAGON MEET AT AT&T

TWO REMINISCENCES

Charles Lee: "I first met Jeff Ganek at AT&T in 1985, when I accepted a consulting assignment in corporate development there. His boss, a Chinese-American woman named Dr. Lilly Lai, introduced me to Jeff as someone who had previously worked at AT&T and would help him in his work. Jeff, then in his early 30s, had just graduated from business school; AT&T was his first job with a major corporation. He struck me as being a typical young MBA—arrogant and abrasive, with a challenging 'who needs you' manner and a total ignorance of global business. I thought he resented me and felt that a Chinese-American clique spearheaded by a woman was seeking to victimize him."

Jeff Ganek: "I first met Charles Lee when I was a division manager for corporate development. Into my office walks this broad-thinking guy who was intent upon realizing a global telecom strategy when most people still thought of AT&T as a public utility. He was so different from anyone else, a breath of fresh air. One of the first things out of his mouth was something about raising a $36 million venture capital fund and becoming a "bridge" between the East and the West. I thought it sounded more than a little grandiose—a multi-million-dollar pipe dream. Then he began a shameless articulation of what were clearly the right directions for the company. I was captivated."

Jeff and I have very different recollections of our first meeting some 18 years ago—a meeting that set in motion a series of events still continuing today. Our preconceptions when we first met could not have been more different. I saw Jeff as a typical Cowboy MBA of the sort I had encountered many times before—someone who readily resented people of Chinese descent. Without ever consciously realizing it, I had fallen into the trap of reacting to him the way a Dragon might when faced with a group of American businesspeople. In reality, my preconceptions were totally wrong—except that I was right about his lack of global knowledge at that time. Jeff saw me not as a member of the gang of two but rather as a wild-eyed visionary, which was closer to the mark.

Despite our comic initial misunderstandings of one another, we made a good pair—a Cowboy and a Dragon working together to transform a fallen giant. The story of our meeting illustrates the negative power of preconceptions: If we had each hardened our initial impression, arrogant Cowboy and pie-eyed visionary, nothing could have happened between us. Instead, we came close to pulling off the mergers and acquisitions stroke of the century.

We developed a list of the major corporations that AT&T might acquire: DEC, Wang Labs, Apple, Microsoft, and ITT. ITT was in a post-Geneen breakup phase and appeared to us to offer the best opportunity. Jeff quickly ran out the numbers and determined that the individual pieces of the ITT conglomerate empire exceeded the value of the existing organization. AT&T could buy ITT, peddle everything non-telecom, and end up with the first truly global telecom business!

TALL CHIMNEYS OF POWER

Jeff directed our proposal to the very top of AT&T management. My own contacts enabled me to do the same within ITT. Together we worked the idea up the tall chimneys of power in both organizations. Of course, you already know that our idea did not succeed. You probably don't know that ITT's top management was very receptive; AT&T's executives became intrigued by the idea but didn't feel they had either the time or the capability to manage such a global business. They still used public utility thinking.

CHAPTER THREE

How Cowboys View Dragons

Americans have little compelling interest in China—an unstudied apathy. When Americans do regard the Chinese, they think of three things: *food*, *history*, and *personal reserve*. The Cowboy view of Dragons encompasses to some degree the four aspects of cultural awareness—cultural/traditional, social/pop cultural, political, and economic—but Americans see China in straightforward black and white, with little shading or subtlety, where Dragons watch America in living Technicolor, through a Hollywood lens.

FOOD FOR THOUGHT

Chinese has become our second most popular ethnic food, Italian being number one. Unfortunately, Americans generally know little about the rich history and significance behind Chinese food culture. The food itself may be colorful, but the Cowboy view of Chinese food has a monochromatic look to it.

Cowboys don't see what the Chinese are doing with food, because the two peoples have very different lenses for viewing it. For Cowboys, Chinese food gets consumed just like any other item in a consumer society. The Chinese find the idea of "consuming" food appalling; in China, food gets eaten as an age-old family ritual heavily loaded with symbolic meaning. Cowboys tend to worry a lot about caloric content and precise nutritional value, all of which puzzles Dragons, who don't understand the West's fractionating thought.

We all eat like we think: Cowboys divide food into categories and count calories; Dragons seek balance and harmony.

A Beef Delicacy

For thousands of years, the Chinese have favored eating a balanced diet. Taoist philosophy teaches the importance of the natural balance deriving from eating meat and vegetables. You are what you eat in Chinese thought. Here is an example of what I mean. One day, an American executive for a firm I advised on Asian business development—let's call him Tom—accompanied me and our Chinese hosts to a Beijing banquet at a Chinese restaurant, of course. Twelve courses had been ordered, including a highly regarded Chinese delicacy that consisted of the male cow's sex organ.

Now the Chinese show hospitality by serving you personally. Tom really liked this dish; our hosts found this quite amusing and gave him more and then even more. "Charles," he whispered to me, "this is really good. What is it?" "Well, Tom, this is a very expensive Chinese delicacy. It is beef dick." Then I explained to him that the Chinese believe that whatever part of an animal you eat helps your human counterpart, so eating this delicacy strengthens your sex organ. When Tom went home, with a laugh he related the story to his wife. She thought for a moment and said, "How long does it take to work?" So you see, I am learning American-style humor.

BACKING THE WRONG HORSE: A HISTORY LESSON

Americans generally know that China has a long history, but they tend to think that real civilization began in Europe, or perhaps that European civilization itself originated in ancient Greece or in the Middle East. Americans also tend to think of the Western world as the home of philosophy, not recognizing that Chinese philosophy beginning with Confucianism dates back as far as Socrates and Plato. The Chinese Enlightenment began when Europeans still lived in huts.

Americans also point to China's recent Communist government as a major fact of its history. This, of course, is true but by itself fails to give due recognition to the continuing impact of tradition on Chinese society and on Chinese communism itself. China has had for several millennia a centralized, hierarchical form of government symbolized by its numerous, emperor-led dynasties. The Chinese Communists adopted many aspects of Chinese ruling tradition in order to reunify the country following World War II. Cowboys rarely know anything about the China predating Communist rule. Cowboys also have an unremittingly black view of Chinese communism. For Dragons, Chairman Mao reestablished the ancient rule of the emperors.

Dragons know that Mao made serious overtures to America just at the end of World War II. President Roosevelt did not reply. The Cowboys didn't "lose China" to the Communists; America simply backed the wrong horse.

ORIENTAL SECRECY

Chinese reserve, or politeness, really brings out the Cowboy in Americans. The Cowboy spirit tends to see Dragons as reserved in behavior, autocratic, hardworking . . . and *secretive*. Cowboys, of course, see Americans as transparently open and trustworthy, so they tend to look on the apparently secretive Chinese with suspicion. Look what happens: Cowboys get told by Western "experts" that the Chinese are inward looking and secretive, so a natural Chinese reserve and deference gets mistaken for some form of dark distrust of Westerners—the black power of preconceptions.

Why? Westerners have been taught to say what is on their minds. Cowboys are open and candid about their thoughts, even to expressing thoughts that are a little "off color." Americans may even follow the belief from Western psychology that it is unhealthy to "repress" thoughts that are not "nice." The Chinese have been taught that what matters most in life is what you do, not what you think. Respect for social harmony prevents the Chinese from expressing disharmonious thoughts, especially sexually explicit ones. For an individual Chinese, having all kinds of really kinky thoughts is all right and perfectly healthy, so long as you don't speak them or act them out in public. No sex talk please, we're Chinese.

In addition to having a somewhat simplistic understanding of China, Cowboys also miss the point of a number of basic Chinese cultural facts of life.

MISPERCEPTION: THE WHOLE MEANING OF FOOD

Western misperceptions about China begin with food. All food in China gets prepared in bite-sized pieces in the kitchen, because food can then be eaten without any "barbarian" chopping and slicing away at big chunks, which would be inelegant and impolite. The whole activity of eating assumes a communal, ritual quality in which due deference to elders and superiors gets displayed. Almost all of this ritual gets lost on Americans, who inevitably make many offensive blunders. The differences in the way Cowboys and Dragons regard food appears in Figure 3.1.

Cowboys use cutting implements at the table because their ancestors included landed lords who loved the hunt. Dragons forbid cutting implements at the table because their ancestors honored scholars.

Chopsticks symbolize the loving delicacy with which the Chinese regard food; they are symbolically the very slender extensions of fingers. A fork has four prongs, or perhaps three, but a chopstick has only one. A pair of chopsticks makes a collective, symbolizing a whole human being. The Chinese symbol for a human being is two brush strokes, one longer than the other, meaning that it takes a man and woman to make completeness. Chopsticks given as wedding presents symbolize that now a couple has united; the gift is two pairs of chopsticks, one for her and one for him. Chopsticks are very economical, used over and over again; each person has his or her own personal pair at home. When people stop by at mealtime, Dragons say, "Add another pair of chopsticks."

Traditionally, family meals get partaken at a round table, with perhaps 10 to 12 extended family members present. Very often, three generations of the same family dine together. Even though the table is round, the seating has a customary order that relates to the head of the family, who sits at the head of the round table.

Now you may jump to the conclusion that I speak in error here: Round tables have no heads! This is true of round tables as far as it goes. The Chinese, however, designate as the table's "head" the chair that directly faces the door; facing the door indicates that you can see any danger coming. Also, food gets served through the door, and you are seated away from the serving of food—the honorable seat.

The round table itself symbolizes wholeness, togetherness, sharing, socializing, and relaxing. All dishes get placed in the middle of the table. Us-

FIGURE 3.1   How Cowboys and Dragons Regard Food

Cowboys	Dragons
Want food served immediately	Want to sit, visit, and sip tea before meal
Eat rapidly	Eat slowly for a time, visit, then eat slowly again
Lean back and talk over coffee	Finish eating, get up and leave
Eat for individual nourishment and pleasure	Eat for group pleasure and to relax and build *guanxi* and *mainzi* (See Chapters 13 and 14.)

ing chopsticks, everybody picks food from the same source in the center, and all food is shared. Cowboys unconsciously experience something of this when dining in Chinese restaurants, because almost all Americans order a number of Chinese dishes and share them. I don't know of any Western-style restaurants where communal eating gets regularly practiced.

MISPERCEPTION: THE HISTORY OF DRAGON CREATIVITY

Because China fell behind the Western world in technological progress beginning in about the 16th century, Cowboys tend to see Dragons as lacking creativity and innovation. Cowboys mistake the Dragons' impoverished recent past for all of Dragon history. The thinking is simple: These people are backward; they must not be very clever.

Because Cowboys have been told about the unremitting drudgery of life and work in China, they fail to see the underlying creativity, adaptability, and sheer survival capabilities of the Chinese people. Cowboys know how to accomplish a lot while using up a lot of resources. Dragons know how to make a few resources go very far. Cowboys associate creativity with unbounded freedom, so they overlook creativity when it is bounded by necessity.

Survival of the Fittest

I know about survival firsthand, for I lived my earliest years on mainland China during the Japanese invasion, a time when my parents were both police officials in CHIANG Kai-shek's government. Survival was everything for us, and we became very clever at survival strategies. Then we moved to Taiwan, a very dangerous and exposed position for many years. Throughout all of our experiences, we relied on the traditional three sources among the Chinese for keeping life and limb together: a survival mentality, the family concept, and self-sufficiency. We Chinese have been adaptable survivors for literally millennia.

The Business of Names: Cowboys find Chinese names very confusing because Dragons give their *last* name first. To make things worse, Cowboys are never sure whether a Chinese name has already been reversed, into the Western style. To help out in this regard, I have placed a Dragon's last, or family, name first, in capital letters. In America, we call CHIANG Kai-shek "Mr. Chiang." I explain more about the topic of Dragon names in the Quick Tips section.

MISPERCEPTION: THE LACK OF INDIVIDUALISM

Going hand in hand with the Cowboy misperception of Chinese creativity is the matter of the individual. To Cowboys, the individual Dragon appears faceless. Cowboys frequently see Chinese devotion to family and work unit relationships as slavish and confining. In reality, Dragons know that the lifelong relationships they keep may literally make the difference between life and death. Family also creates obligations for achievement; no Dragon wishes to let family elders down by being anything less than he or she can be.

It is therefore not true that in China the individual has neither identity nor value. Rather, it is true that historically in China the environment has carried many threats to each family, so that individual Chinese have needed the support and security of all other family members. In return, Dragons recognize the importance of reciprocal obligations. Each family member must support the others throughout a lifetime. The same practice carries over to the community and the work group, where mutual obligation also dominates. Individual freedom is a luxury few Chinese can afford or would even want, except among the rootless, younger, urban Chinese.

This manner of relating to family and clan does not hinder Chinese creativity or achievement. Look what happens when Dragons live outside mainland China in less authoritative environments. They still keep their deep respect for reciprocal obligations, but they also become fantastically successful professionals and entrepreneurs once their human energy gets more fully released. Few Cowboys recognize this, but the Chinese not only make up the world's largest immigrant body, but they are also the most successful by many measures. Sadly, they are often hated for their hard-earned wealth.

Over the past ten years, the British *Economist* magazine has published a number of fine articles on Chinese expatriate entrepreneurs and family-run businesses. Have a look at the *Economist* Web site.

COMMON GROUND

This matter of striving for achievement can become a genuine common meeting ground for Cowboys and Dragons. "Be all that you can be!" America's army surrogate parent proudly proclaims to young Cowboys. Dragon families wish the same for their children. Many young Cowboys now receive the discipline and encouragement necessary for success within the nation's armed forces. Corporations love to hire ex-servicemen and women for their leadership and team-building abilities. Of course, parents in America also desire the best for their children—that they might find happiness and success. Because the environment is different, Cowboys frequently learn in other institutions what Dragons learn at home.

Underneath the surface differences, the parents of both Cowboys and Dragons want the best for their children. And we are both very hardworking peoples. So you see, we are not so totally different after all.

CERTAIN COWBOY PERCEPTIONS OF DRAGONS

- *They all look alike.* Westerners often say this about the Chinese. The funny thing is that the Chinese say exactly the same thing about Westerners! We each have developed perceptions that selectively discriminate very finely, with regard to our own people. We lack such selective perception with regard to people from the other land, and that helps explain why we Westerners find the Chinese so "inscrutable." Once Cowboys and Dragons spend a little time together, we each begin to notice how unique each individual from the other land really is.

- *They are very poor and backward.* Although this is true from an affluent Western perspective, the Chinese don't say this about themselves. Rather, they say that they are better off than before—which is also true. Once more, there is no one truth about this matter, just two differing perspectives. What both Cowboys and Dragons hold in common is that we are all better off than before.

- *They are all the same.* Westerners believe that all Easterners are pretty much the same—that the peoples of the East are homogeneous. This also turns out to be quite untrue. Instead, the supposedly homogeneous population of the East turns out to have a very heterogeneous nature. When Cowboys say that everyone in the East is the same, they risk offending their Eastern hosts. Here is a story that illustrates what I mean, as well as our very different senses of humor. It seems that young GIs in Vietnam during the war often went out on the town to meet locals. Not being able to distinguish Easterners by their national origin, young GIs often asked, "Hey, what 'nese' are you anyway?" By that, the GI meant, "Are you Vietnamese, Chinese, or maybe even Japanese?" The local people didn't find that very funny, not understanding American bantering. So a Vietnamese once replied to a GI: "What 'key' are *you?*" The GI replied, "What do you mean?" "Well, are you a monkey, a donkey, or a Yankee?" The GI got very mad. We can all become alike by accepting our differences. China, like America, is a great melting pot—or perhaps we are both huge mosaics.

- *"They" are a huge new market for our products.* The Chinese are still leery of American-style consumption driven by marketing campaigns, although the younger generation finds everything American most appealing. Chinese leaders see American forays in the context of earlier Western invasions; they don't wish to hand over markets and get nothing for China in return. Once more, China is not a homogeneous country of 1 billion people speaking the same language, open to a one-size-fits-all marketing campaign. In reality, 75 percent of all Chinese are farmers, not city dwellers, and they engage in subsistence living. They will not demand American consumer goods, so the market is not so big as many Cowboys think. The Chinese speak over 100 different dialects; two Chinese people from different states can read the same message, but they cannot understand each other's speech! A further warning: the Chinese don't buy from somebody they don't already know very well.

RECOMMENDATIONS

1. *Do not* approach China from the narrow point of view of gaining quick access to a "huge market" or to "cheap labor." You will only multiply your chances for failure.
2. *Do not* engage in criticisms of "backward" China or the Chinese form of government. You will offend your Chinese counterparts in ways that you won't even understand.
3. *Do* get to know your Chinese counterparts as individuals. Put your personal relationships ahead of any business dealings. Remember that in China business follows relationships, not the other way around.

CHAPTER FOUR

What Happens When Cowboys and Dragons Meet

A MOST LIKELY OUTCOME

The Cowboy team faces a business meeting with a group of Dragons in a few months. The Americans want the Chinese to manufacture for them; the Chinese want to increase local employment. What does each side do to prepare for the meeting? The Cowboy side concentrates on the business proposal—what can we pay and still make a targeted profit? The Cowboys also hire a corporate consultant to coach them on how they should behave toward the Chinese during the trip. The consultant is invariably a Westerner peddling Western perceptions of Eastern ways. Such consultants work as stereotype enforcers.

Unknown to the Cowboys, the Chinese also carefully prepare for the meeting—by finding out everything they can about the American company's previous involvement in the East and about how to do business with these foreigners. They use other Chinese as de facto consultants. Of course, the other Chinese tell them what they want to hear.

Both sides concentrate on what they do best. Neither side, however, prepares by studying a critical question: *What does the other side believe about us?* Instead, each side considers only certain preconceptions about the other party. It never even enters anyone's mind that the other party might also hold some damning preconceptions about us, the good guys. Both sides fly blind into bad weather.

> Everybody prepares for a business meeting by doing what each does best. Instead, also prepare by practicing what you do worst.

When the two parties meet, the Cowboys push for a quick result. Let's nail down a firm agreement as soon as possible, before they have a chance to back out or demand more. We know that the Dragons cannot be trusted. They're shifty Orientals.

The Dragons listen with an ear finely tuned by past grievances. They know that the Cowboys want to make quick, short-term profits. They have also been told that Cowboys lack patience: Hold out, and you can always get a better deal. Above all else, the Cowboys have no concern for the common good as we do. They are all greedy.

> The most important question about the other party to a business deal is not: What are they like? The most important question is: What does the other party think we are like?

As the meeting goes on, each side becomes more confirmed in its pre-conceptions about the other: The Americans *are* so pushy, so eager; in their great greed, they only want us for our cheap labor. The Chinese are not open and honest; no matter what we offer, they become *evasive;* they have something to hide. In this charade, distrust merely grows. Every word and movement confirms each side's preconceptions of the other. The deal eventually evaporates. It is so easy to find what you look for.

THE OTHER WAY

If each side learns something about how the other side regards it, the charade can stop. As a simple example, Chinese businessmen frequently believe that their American counterparts are very greedy. An American businessman who knows this can find a chance to explain the pressures he faces to his Chinese counterpart. For the American, the pressure to make short-term profits comes from both his company and the stock market. Explain this, and the Chinese can then understand that Americans live under pressure just as they do—it's just a different kind of pressure.

The Chinese, in turn, feel pressure to meet all of the joint obligations of membership in a work unit—something the Chinese leader may then explain to the American. Now, each leader has a better understanding of what motivates his counterpart's behavior. As a divisive issue, greed has now been disarmed, as has evasiveness.

THE THREE HOW QUESTIONS

Using this better way to disarm preconceptions means that each side has to work at what it does worst. Fortunately, a simple method exists for learning how to do this. Answer each of the following three questions:

1. How do I see myself?
2. How do I see the other party?
3. How does the other party see me?

The first two questions are fairly easy; the third can be difficult—especially for people in the West. Cowboys believe that other people see them exactly as they see themselves.

The third question is in reality very Eastern. Dragons want to know how other Chinese perceive them, because obtaining the good will of others makes up an important part of each Dragon's personal survival strategy. For the Chinese, survival does not come from the trigger end of a gun; Cowboys traditionally carried a Colt Peacemaker.

How Cowboys and Dragons Answer

I have found over many years of living in America that Cowboy entrepreneurs describe themselves in terms of three major attributes: *ingenuity, freedom of action and openness,* and *adventuresomeness.* These attributes contribute to the Cowboys' ability to accomplish great things in little time. Cowboys view their Chinese counterparts as being just the opposite— slavish copiers who are unimaginative, secretive, and frightened of risk. Furthermore, the Chinese must know exactly who we are as well, because we are so open about it. And, of course, in all of our perceptions we are right.

Dragons see themselves in terms of three major attributes also: *harmony* (within oneself and with family, community, society, nation, and world), *loyalty* (to the same entities, in reverse order), and *diligence* (working hard, both physically and intellectually). So Americans do things in meetings that upset the Chinese deeply; they are so disrespectful, the Dragons feel.

For example, when the Americans make a presentation to the Chinese, more than one Cowboy speaks; maybe all do. Sometimes, individual Cowboys even contradict one another or, worse yet, their leader. Cowboys see all of this as positive. It tells the other party that we are sponta-

> There is no way that an American can be truly courteous in the Chinese manner. Cowboys can, however, avoid outright rudeness. For instance, don't expect the Chinese to speak English!

neous, open, and very creative, constantly making improvements on what we do. Dragons don't see it in this light. They see the Cowboys as lacking respect for harmony within their work unit and for their leader. They may work very hard, but, unlike us, they are destructive. And, of course, the Dragons are sure that they are right.

Neither side normally answers the third question, the tough one: How does the other party see us? Righteousness gets in the way.

THE MAGICAL WHY

The same human nature resides inside Dragons and Cowboys alike. Neither party's members really want to know what the foreigners think of them, because everyone secretly assumes it is probably both bad and wrong. When the Cowboys learn that the Dragons think they are very greedy, the natural reaction is anger at being wronged. The same emotion gets generated when Dragons learn that Cowboys feel they are shifty. Scratch our skin, and we both bleed.

Both sides can become stuck at this point: We have taken the effort to learn what the other side believes about us, and we are furious about it. Now we can either remain stuck in our anger or get out of it by asking the simple, magical question: *Why?* No preconception can stand up for very long against why.

For example, *why* do Dragons appear so shifty and evasive? In the Cowboys' world, everyone possesses a great deal of individual freedom and may give a quick answer. In the Dragons' world, no one may answer quickly because everyone has a personal responsibility for maintaining group harmony. So before arriving at any decision, everyone involved must be consulted. Individual freedom and group harmony cannot peacefully coexist.

Why are Dragons so afraid to take risks? Our American legal system shifts much of the burden of failure from the entrepreneur to financial institutions that are better able to bear the risk. Cowboys become very freewheeling with other people's money, and little shame attaches itself to bankruptcy. Nothing like this exists in China. Failure strikes a work

> If you receive a "fast yes" from a younger Dragon, beware! That Dragon may have adopted American decision-making ways without the *guanxi* "clout" to carry the decision through.

unit directly and devastates social harmony. Great shame attaches to failure. Risk taking relates directly to consequences.

Why are Cowboys so advanced technologically and Dragons so backward? This question, of course, goes very deeply into each nation's history. *The Chinese invented advanced technology* but then slowly, as a nation, lost the ability to innovate. America grew to adolescence as a nation of tinkerers and inventors and then became the global high-technology superpower. *Why* did invention shift worlds?

Cowboys frequently attribute the difference to the wrong cause: native intelligence. Although the total answer has too much complexity to develop here, my own background as a venture capitalist suggests one partial response: Cowboys innovate so well because they can get very rich doing it. Dragons, on the other hand, ceased to innovate when the dynastic rulers withdrew recognition and rewards and chose to emphasize social harmony over potentially disruptive social changes deriving from innovation. When Chinese entrepreneurs today have the same chances as their Western counterparts to grow rich, they innovate just as successfully. It is always dangerous to believe that you are smarter than your competition.

> Creativity comes less from genetics than from external rewards. Offer a reward, and even a very average IQ can suddenly yield highly creative solutions to problems.

The Socratic *Why* and the Confucian *What*

One why question frequently begs another. *Why* did Chinese society develop around social harmony and Western society around individualism? Much of Part Two addresses this basic question; this chapter begins by simply observing what the two seminal thinkers, West and East, had to say. Socrates believed that everyone already knew the answers to many questions about life; he used the "Socratic why" to draw out what people already knew. Socratic questioning led the West to discover personally disinterested, cause-and-effect thinking.

In contrast, Confucius wanted to know what could bring peace among warring clans; he used the "Confucian what" to observe and discover what worked as a practical matter. Confucian empirical observation led to relational thinking. The Chinese still emphasize "what" questions through cultural training: Parents require obedience and deemphasize "why" questions. Why challenges authority.

Ask a Cowboy and then a Dragon this simple, Socratic question: Why does the sun rise in the East and set in the West? The Cowboy will answer with an explanation of the Copernican solar system—cause and effect. The Dragon will answer, "The sun has always done so in the past, does so now, and will do so in the future"—empirical observation. Don't ask *why* in China because you won't get an answer.

SAND TRAPS IN THE EAST-WEST GAME OF BUSINESS AND HOW TO AVOID THEM

- *Preconceptions* can absolutely kill your game. Get rid of them.
- *The two worst sorts of preconceptions:* (1) what I believe, in ignorance, about the other party; (2) what I believe, in ignorance, that the other party believes about me. For example, Cowboys frequently fall into the trap of believing that Dragons are actually devious and think that Cowboys are direct and up front. Neither happens to be true.
- *The best way to disarm damaging preconceptions:* Develop honest answers to the three *hows: How* do I see myself? *How* do I see the other party? *How* does the other party see me? The third how is by far the toughest but most important. Cowboys believe that the other side sees them exactly as they themselves think they are—and that's simply not true.
- *The truth frequently hurts.* When you learn how the other party sees you, expect to become deeply hurt and righteously angry. For example, the Chinese think that Cowboys are selfish and greedy. That hurts.

RECOMMENDATIONS FOR IMPROVING YOUR GAME

1. *Practice what you do worst.* Everybody works at developing a great presentation; few people work at understanding how the other side regards them. International business is like golf; the approach shots usually matter more than a great drive.
2. *Beware of a "fast yes."* Expect the Chinese to take a lot of time in reaching decisions. After all, they use consensus decision making, and consensus takes time to reach. If you get a quick, positive decision, allow for the possibility that a Dragon has overstepped some invisible boundaries and may not be able to back up the yes with actions.
3. *Never underestimate your counterparts.* China may be relatively backward, but that does not mean that the Chinese are not as smart as Americans. Instead, always assume that your counterparts are at least as smart as you.
4. *The magical why.* The best way to deal with hurt feelings is to begin using the magical why: Why does the other party believe this or that about me? When you can answer this question, you can then explain to the other party why you behave the way you do. When each side understands the other side's organizational imperatives lying behind its own cultural preconceptions, a real relationship can begin to grow. Being real and honest builds a foundation for doing business together.

COWBOY TRYING TO BE HUMBLE
A TELECOM SAGA

A journey of a thousand miles begins with a single step.
—AN OLD CHINESE PROVERB

During the early 1990s, a number of hotshot American telecom companies charged into the Chinese IT (Information Technology) industry. When the dust settled, the results certainly benefited the Chinese, but more Cowboy companies came up losers than winners. This is the improbable story of one of the winners— a story that began in 1991 at the headquarters of a huge American telecom outfit and ended three years later on Christmas Day 1994 on the 36th floor of the Shanghai Hilton half a world away. (The names, company names, and other details have been changed to protect the sensitive.)

The Cowboy hero of the story—let us call him Gary "Coop" Cooper—first got involved in a China deal while working for TCA (Telecom Corporation of America) as its Marketing VP. Coop was a stocky, strongly built guy, who actually wore blue jeans and cowboy boots to informal business meetings, and sometimes even a cowboy hat! For formal business occasions, he always dressed impeccably in a deep-blue, well-tailored business suit. Nobody ever doubted that he was The Boss. He was a guy who always rode tall in the saddle, and never knuckled under to any man.

The TCA Corporate Development VP had me under contract as what might be called a "hired gun" to help the company "open up" the Chinese market. At first, Coop wanted to blow off my introductory meetings: "I don't need to meet with this Chinese-American guy. Hell, I already know more than most Americans about how to do business in China—certainly more than anyone at TCA, and more than anyone TCA's gonna bring in here."

"Coop, maybe you ought to go anyway," his right-hand man had pleaded. "Top management is really pushing this China thing."

"Oh, hell! All right, I'll go."

After our initial meetings, Coop became my strongest supporter. We came to share the belief that each side needed to learn a lot about the other before we could successfully do a Chinese-American joint venture. I made contact with a number of promising Chinese agencies—including SSTIC (Shanghai Science and Technology Investment Corporation). Things looked very good, until another American firm made Coop an offer he could not refuse. His replacement then decided to ignore my advice and make a decidedly American-style, "take it or leave it" presentation to his Chinese counterparts at SSTIC. "We'll study it very carefully," they replied—a "soft no." My international business diplomacy days seemed to reach an end.

Then, I got a call from Coop. A startup named TASS (TransAtlantic Satellite Services) had hired him as VP for Asian Operations—a totally new position as the company had no operations in Asia. "Charles, I want to reopen negotiations with the Chinese. Could you help me?" I agreed, and became once more a most unlikely Cowboy hired gun—slender and obviously of Chinese ancestry.

Our first problem involved Chairman Liu of SSTIC, a real hard-core communist technocrat who had earned a Ph.D. in Russia. Dr. Liu's father had attended Columbia University, as had his Number One daughter. His wife is a professor. Coming from a prominent and very cosmopolitan Shanghai family, he had once been a vice mayor of the city with authority over science, technology, and cultural affairs. He had begun negotiating with TCA, one of the biggest U.S. telecom outfits; now we had to persuade him to trust one of the smallest!

I told Coop that when we met with Dr. Liu he had to play humble Cowboy. At that stage, Coop had a pretty neutral attitude toward the Chinese. He had never formed any real friendships with them, but he respected their technical capabilities and willingness to learn. Dr. Liu appeared in a well-tailored western-style business suit for our meeting. He had been a weightlifter as a younger man, and looked even stockier than Coop. He also appeared very stunned when we told him that we now worked for a little start-up company, rather than for giant TCA. "TASS! What is that!" he exploded.

The change offended him deeply, because of his Chinese sense for betrayal of *danwei*—the basic Chinese organizational unit (see Chapter 15). Then, we sat down together, and Coop began. As he spoke, he clasped his hands in front of him, and rocked back and forth in his chair, leaning forward as he made major points. I translated. It went something like: " First, I need to acknowledge the mistakes that the previous American management team made in negotiating with you . . . . Second, I need to confess that I don't know at all how to do business in China. But I am willing to learn . . . . I need to learn what your needs are, so that I can assess what we can do for you."

All the Chinese present nodded approval, following Chairman Liu's lead. The humble act worked pretty well, although the Chinese found its sincerity a bit suspect. Then, I had Coop tell them that TASS had venture capital funding. "Oh, venture capital!" Dr. Liu had sent young Chinese to study the American venture capital industry, and had formed a favorable opinion of it. He positively beamed his approval.

Everything was okay—until a little later TASS reorganized as WSL (World Satellite Links). "What! You were TCA, then TASS, and now you are WSL! What is going on?" Chairman Liu flew into a passion, and we flew once more to China. Coop replayed Cowboy trying to be humble. I had him explain to Dr. Liu that WSL was the renamed TASS and that we now had a lot of money coming from a huge venture group. "Oh, more venture capital!" The Chairman approved. We had successfully switched him twice.

Through a series of follow-up meetings, things began to look very good for our new joint venture called SVC (Shanghai VSAT Company). We ran a series of "getting to know you" meetings, in both China and America. The Chinese hosted us in Beijing, highlighted by a trip to the Forbidden City. We also took in the Chinese opera and made a journey to the Great Wall. Coop took the Chinese team on a tour of New York, where the New York Stock Exchange was the highlight (we arranged a personalized tour by the NYSE Chairman). We also brought the Chinese to Washington D.C. and to an operating facility in California. Coop hosted a dinner for them in his home—a way to show developing friendship and respect.

Everything looked right on track until our guys decided they didn't want to keep a November meeting already scheduled for Shanghai—too close to the

Thanksgiving holiday—so the Cowboys unilaterally canceled. The first I knew of it came when I got a call telling me the whole deal was off; the Chinese were pulling out, deeply offended.

> Cowboys act unilaterally; Dragons consult first. Cowboys are thick-skinned; Dragons are thin-skinned when "face" is involved.

To save the deal, I told Coop there was only one thing we could do: Get on the next airplane to Shanghai. That flight happened to be on Christmas Eve. "Coop, when we see Chairman Liu, we need to do only one thing: apologize." Twenty hours later, we met Chairman Liu in the executive dining room at the top of the Shanghai Hilton. Coop made a humble personal apology, explaining to Dr. Liu that Thanksgiving was a very important American holiday, and that we had come to see him on an even more important holiday to set things right. He then explained the nature of both holidays, but especially Christmas. When Chairman Liu realized we had both given up such important personal time with our families to come to China, he was very impressed. Our negotiations would proceed to a happy conclusion. Of course, Coop, the quintessential American Cowboy, didn't tell Chairman Liu that he himself happened to be Jewish.

The Moral of the Story: When dealing with the Chinese, you cannot be too polite or considerate of the other party. An apology to a Dragon is not "eating humble pie" as it is for a Cowboy. It is a highly esteemed, daily means of assuring social harmony.

PART TWO

Cultural Differences: The Three Ts Plus One

How can I really know you, unless I understand where you come from? Cowboys and Dragons alike behave in certain ways determined by thousands of years of separate cultural development. This part of *Cowboys and Dragons* provides a whistle-stop tour of the three general areas contributing the most to our cultural differences: *tradition, time,* and *thought.*

Consider the way Cowboys and Dragons climb stairs. Americans charge up stairs like Teddy Roosevelt at San Juan Hill. Unless they are very fit or youthful, they stop part of the way up, panting to catch their breath. The Chinese go up stairs slowly and deliberately, without pausing until they reach the top. The different behaviors involve all three Ts—tradition, time, and thought. The approach to stairs symbolizes the approach to life.

We have been apart a long time, but now East and West are coming together more and more. Each world has begun to have profound influences upon the other. The three Ts no longer suffice to describe our differences, so we must add a fourth: *transition.* The huge question we face is, Where will transition lead us?

CHAPTER FIVE

Tradition
WHERE THE DIFFERENCES BEGAN

RAIDERS OF THE CENTRAL KINGDOMS

A native rider mounted on a rugged stallion looks across the bleak desert landscape far into the distance. No patrols appear along the rough trail connecting two fortresses some ten miles apart. The raid can go forward. The raiding party knifes its way across the border and rides far into settled country. A bloody several days' work lies ahead.

Reaching a farming community, the raiders easily subdue the sedentary peasants, killing all the males. Then they burn the settlement to the ground, taking women and children captive with them, and cattle. The risks now increase. Will they avoid the patrols while returning home, or will they be forced to kill their captives and run for it? Their fortune holds, and they reach a nomadic home village. Some cattle they keep, others they slaughter and eat. They rape the women and enslave both them and their children. Some women make replacement wives. Appetites get fed; moveable wealth increases.

A scene from the old Wild West? By no means. The scenario takes place in northern China some 2,000 years before the emergence of mounted Native Americans and Western Cowboys. Mongols make up the native raiding party. The agrarian peasants are Han, early Chinese who have moved northward from the original heartland of what will become the Chinese Empire. The Mongol raiders threaten an already ancient, feudal Chinese civilization whose origins go back a thousand more years. For the first time in history, Cowboys and Dragons meet.

Cowboys are raiders by nature; Dragons are growers.

Ancient Roots for Two Traditions

Cowboy and Dragon behaviors, then, go back very far. The first Cowboys, the ancient mounted nomads of the steppes, displayed deeply polarized behaviors—caring for cattle and raiding for profit—but all the while restless. Cowboys have always found strength in the mastery of the physical environment, using force when required. Dragon behavior developed from the desire for protection against such raiders. The Dragon itself symbolizes the power of people living in civil society to overcome the foreigner. Dragon distrust runs deep.

Who finally conquered whom? Invading Mongols intermarried with the Han and became absorbed by Chinese culture. Superior Chinese administrative skills eventually led the Mongols to invite Chinese rule into their lands. The Dragons co-opted Cowboy raw power and ruled. Even the last Chinese dynasty, founded by a Manchurian family, controlled China in a thoroughly Chinese manner. Only one question remains: Where did the Chinese administrative brilliance come from?

The Emperor Strikes Back

Several hundred years after the Mongol raids began, a Chinese warlord would unify significant parts of feudal northern China. He would connect the frontier fortresses to create the Great Wall. He would see his vast empire hampered by incompatible systems for writing and enforce written compatibility on a large land by ruthlessly burning books and rewriting everything anew in a single language. He would standardize weights and measures as well, to make for more efficient internal trade—and tax collection. Never forget taxes.

Millions would die in his reforms, but a single identity for all the Chinese would be forged. He would be named QIN SHIHUANG—the first Emperor of the land directly below Heaven. The first Emperor came to be perceived as an earthly god, the son of a primordial heavenly god who opened the sky and formed the earth, and the Emperor rode a dragon down to earth to rule. China was the central point or pillar of the earth: China, or *Zhong Guo,* literally means "The Central or Middle Kingdom."

The Chinese began to look inward and still do today. After all, if you're born under the "Eye of Heaven," why look anywhere else?

> To this day, even though the Chinese speak many different dialects whose speakers cannot comprehend one another, written Chinese is understood by everyone.

The first Emperor's legitimacy, termed the *Mandate of Heaven,* derived from his descent from Heaven on the dragon. His immediate successors ascended to the imperial throne by birthright, in an orderly, harmonious manner—the Emperor is dead, long live the Emperor! The transfer of power on a ruler's death no longer brought a struggle over the succession—a development that stabbed feudalism in the heart. QIN SHIHUANG killed off Chinese feudalism a thousand years before the Europeans even thought it up.

The Emperors and the Confucian Tradition

Around the time of the Mongolian lawlessness, the scholar-teacher Confucius (K'UNG Fu-Tzu, later latinized by the Jesuits) traveled among the sometimes-warring Han clans, each with a feudal warlord, studying the appearances of conflict and the apparent examples of social harmony. He would eventually conceive the instruction manual for a peaceful, harmonious social order. The actual implementation of his thought would come only some 300 years later—after the first Emperor united China during the third century B.C. The belief that harmony originated in Heaven and descended downward on a Dragon's back through the Emperor, or Son of Heaven, and then to the lowest social orders gave Emperor rule a crucial legitimacy. The Emperor "owned" the empire and regarded his subjects as "children." Confucius and the Dragon civilized China.

> *Zhong he,* or "balanced harmony," does not mean that everybody behaves like the bees in a hive. Confucian harmony achieves a dynamic balance between divergent and often conflicting human demands.

THE CONFUCIAN SOCIAL ORDER

Confucian harmony put scholars or learned men at the top of the social hierarchy. Learned men could administer state affairs with harmony and justice, all based in Confucian teachings. Military men received such low regard that they were grouped with outlaws at the very bottom! Only in tumultuous times did military men rise in regard, and even then the scholar-generals greatly outranked men of mere military ability; perhaps these were the world's first "textbook generals." The one certain thing is that a Chinese general named SUN Tzu did write the first military textbook, *The Art of War.*

The real class division in Chinese society soon appeared—that between the scholars, men who had mastered the classics and passed the civil service entry exams, and everybody else. Even under Chairman Mao, this held true until the Cultural Revolution. The words of Mao simply replaced the teachings of Confucius, or tried to.

In the Confucian order, merchants were regarded as a sterile class, producing nothing by themselves but trading on the sweat of others. Businesspeople still get looked down on in China today. In 18th-century France, the Physiocrats thought up the same idea about merchants as a sterile class. Some ideas are so bad that they are bound to reappear.

In the Confucian order, everybody got educated about the fundamental concept of knowing his or her place in the whole scheme of social relations. A person's place in the overall Harmony of Heaven depended on the *five cardinal relations: Heaven-earth, Emperor-subject, father-son, husband-wife,* and *brother-brother.* Each of these relations involved positions of authority and deference, sometimes of a very subtle nature when the paired relation involved kin or friends. Authority and deference appeared everywhere, which may be why the Chinese do so much bowing.

Chinese individuals lived their lives totally bounded by multiple, paired relations, all within an ascending hierarchy of owed deference and obedience. Brotherly obedience trumped friendship, which in turn got trumped by paternal obedience. The obedience due a father by a son always outweighed marital relations. Ultimate obedience ascended to the Emperor, who in turn is the Son of Heaven. Obedience to the Emperor assumed such an absolute nature that even the last-ruling Manchu Emperor PU Yi could call on an official to commit suicide, and the man would readily do so!

Confucian harmony dominated Chinese government right through the 1911 overthrow of the last Emperor, followed by the brief republican interlude under SUN Yat-sen and the tumult under CHIANG Kai-shek leading to Communist rule in 1949. To the Chinese, the Communists are not the bad guys; they are the latest of many ruling dynasties.

MEANWHILE, BACK IN THE WEST . . .

The developing harmonious world order of the Chinese looked very different from the one around the Mediterranean basin, also about 500 B.C. By that time, a number of ancient empires in the West had already come and gone—due to invasion, conquest, and subsequent forceful overthrow. These competing major civilizations had formed in the Near East and Mediterranean coastal areas, most notably in Egypt and the Fertile Crescent. Clashing kingdoms were the rule.

Many smaller tribes were interspersed along the great civilizations' borders, both East and West. Some, such as the tribes of the steppes, fed off the bigger empires and the East-West trade along the Old Silk Road. Some remained marginalized and stubbornly unconquerable. Three of them changed the Western world forever.

Israel was the first influential small tribe, or collection of tribes, that would ultimately shape the West. The Israelites created the idea of the modern individual as an independent entity apart from social grouping and standing alone in relationship to a supreme deity. They also created the idea of creation itself—the idea that the universe had a beginning out of nothing. From the idea of a beginning came time as we know it in the West. No similar idea developed in China. As a result, Cowboys today think in terms of the future; Dragons conceive of everything in the present.

In China you receive a group identity; in the West, you make your own individual identity.

The first modern man lived in Jerusalem around 800 B.C. He subjugated and ruled over the sometimes warring 12 tribes, living life to the fullest and writing poetry about it. In the process, the Israelite's tribal deity became for him the personal, intimate, living God. He was King David. One of his future progeny—Ruth—became the first modern woman. In the East, no such thing as the psychologically distinct individual in the Western sense would emerge into full light; the East had no equivalent to the Old Testament Prophets or King David or to the teacher Socrates. Where Socrates says "I," Confucius replies "we."

You may wish to read Thomas Cahill's recent book *The Gifts of the Jews: How a Tribe of Desert Nomads Changed the Way Everyone Thinks and Feels*. Of course, "everyone" does not include the Chinese.

The second small tribe, or collection of tribes, to change the West forever was of course Greece. Slightly later than Confucius, Socrates began to study the natural order of things. The Socratic Question—"why?"—would form the basis for all modern Western philosophy and science. Before Socrates, earlier Greek thinkers had laid the foundations for science as we know it. Even the idea itself of a thinker, in the sense of an abstract mental processor divorced from immediate human relationships, stands as a stunning and original Greek achievement—a totally new thing. The Greeks also gave the world an entirely new organizational principle: the city-state ruled by the citizens' vote and by natural law. Dragons rely on gut feeling; beginning with the Greeks, Cowboys think.

PAX ROMANA

The third small tribal group to define the West forever lived and fought with rival tribes in Italy for nearly a millennium. Then it rather suddenly emerged to dominance among competing civilizations. The fledgling Roman Republic had followed the Greek city-states in overturning the rule of the despot for the rule of law executed by citizens. Simultaneously with the unification of feudal China under one Emperor, the small Roman Republic grew by conquest to encompass most of the Mediterranean basin and much of Asia Minor. Roman rule forced a troubled peace on the warring local tribes—*Pax Romana*—just as America does today. The emerging Roman Empire would always be held together more by force than by common culture and beliefs, nor would it ever dominate Israelite and Greek thought. The Romans grabbed an empire where the Chinese grew one.

In some ways, however, Rome resembled China. The succession to imperial power became generally orderly. Innovation flourished as well although probably not so grandly as in China. The social order, too, possessed a hierarchical nature that required deference to authority and obedience: the family gathering around the homestead's sacred hearth to honor the father of the house, seen in China as a microcosm of the grander order of the empire. Yet the Roman Empire contained elements of its own destruction, whereas the Chinese Empire survived similar threats and lasted.

The Romans gave Westerners something that really baffles the Chinese even today: Roman Law. Thanks to Rome, Law trumps everything else in the West. In China, laws exist, but the Ruler says what they are.

THE THREE PILLARS OF CIVILIZATION—EAST AND WEST

I have now traced East and West developments until about 2,000 years ago, far enough to observe how differently the underlying bases for civilization took shape. In reality, every civilization gets upheld by three main pillars: *philosophy, religion,* and *science/material culture.* The West's pillars, however, look totally different from the East's. In philosophy, it is "I" versus "we." In religion, it is one God versus many gods or perhaps no gods at all! In the West, the "I" relates to the "One God"; in the East, people relate to dead ancestors, to the gods, or to nature. Or they relate to the eternal way, absolute reality itself—the *Tao.* Within science and material culture, the West asks *why*—the material cause for every effect; the East asks *what*—the facts from empirical observation. The modern world of the Cowboys stands firmly supported by three classical Greek stone columns; the world of the Dragons rests on three tree trunks growing out of the soil.

COMMERCIAL TRADITIONS—EAST AND WEST

Economic traditions form part of the third pillar, and they, too, look very different in the East and the West, especially once the Western Renaissance began. Imagine for a moment that you have an all-seeing view of the early 15th century. In China, you can watch the Emperor by formal decree bring an end to Chinese international trade, condemning fleets of magnificent ocean-going junks to rot at wharves. The Emperor feels that international trade will threaten the internal harmony of his realm by creating external threats to his authority and by empowering the lowly, sterile merchant class. Everything must revolve around the Chinese capital.

On a local scale, repeated millions of times, a Chinese merchant bows down very low to a neighbor, obsequiously asking for his business. If the merchant is lucky enough, his prostrations may lift his eldest son into the ranks of the civil service, where family fortunes get made. Scholars rule. Sons rise on the backs of their fathers.

Meanwhile, in the Republic of Venice, a rich merchant family enters into a large business deal with a counterpart in France for a shipment of highest-quality Venetian cloth. The French merchant will pay for the cloth with a bill of exchange drawn on a banking house in Luca, Italy. Accounts will be kept in a double-entry bookkeeping system designed to prevent fraudulent behavior on the part of the merchant's counting house employees. The rich Venetian merchant occupies a position of the highest standing in this city of international traders and manufacturers of highest-quality Venetian wares. His sons want nothing more than to succeed him in the family business.

> In the West, time gets kept in zones by longitudinal location; in China, there is only one time—kept in Beijing.

In very simple terms, the social order of the West appears inverted when compared with that of the East. In China, the most highly regarded men were all scholars. Under them came the landlords, peasants, and craftsmen. At the very bottom came the merchants and then the soldiers and outlaws. Among the bottom feeders, the latter stole a lot, and the former did a lot of bowing.

In the West, following the decline of Rome, military men and landed aristocrats, including Churchmen, sat at the top of the social pyramid. Under them came the merchants and scholars, then the craftsmen, and lastly the peasants. Some people in the West felt that the thieves were all at the top.

The inverted social orders have great significance for later historical developments. By emphasizing the scholar-administrator applying the tools of harmony within the empire, China became relatively inward looking and defenseless against later invaders. By stifling foreign trade, China kept its merchant class in perpetual lower-order disgrace. Conversely, the preeminence of military men would eventually bloom in the West into a nasty, warring feudal era. The preeminence of Western traders would lead directly to the Western Commercial and Industrial Revolutions, and in turn to modern Western economies. China would miss these revolutions.

HOW TO SUCCEED IN BUSINESS . . .

Had you lived 500 years ago, what would you have written for a best-seller entitled *How to Succeed in Business by Really Trying Hard?* Had you lived in China, your book would be about the ins and outs of government and how to manipulate rulers to accomplish your goals. Had you lived in the West, your book would emphasize how to transact business under great uncertainty, and how to profit from newly discovered technologies. In the West, your greatest asset would gradually become your people—the brighter, the better. In China, all of the brightest people would already be in the government, taxing you.

THINGS STAY THE SAME—A BUSINESS SCHOOL SUCCESS STORY

I recently learned firsthand that some things never change in business and government. In the fall of 2001, I spoke to an eMBA class at Qinghua University Business School in Beijing. Qinghua is the top engineering school in China, equivalent to MIT in the United States. Prior to my talk on "Bicultural versus Bilingual Business Skills," I gained some background information on the business school. It seems that its current pre-eminence stems directly from its successful graduates and the executive talent of its former Dean—ZHU Rongi. Mr. Zhu ran the school from 1984 until he recently became the Premier of China. In China, scholars still rule!

Mr. Zhu personally put Qinghua on the map as the major rival of the Guanghua Business School of Peking University. (Guanghua is like the Harvard B School, and Peking University is China's Harvard—so you see the nature of the competitive rivalry.) He did so, in part, through his philosophy of whom to admit into his MBA program: only those likely to become the best future business people *for* China—a very Chinese way of thinking. The best Cowboy business schools, of course, admit the most talented *individuals.* Here it is again—the cooperative versus the individual.

Who are these people that Mr. Zhu's philosophy favored? People in their 30s who *already* had experience in Chinese government and who either already had, or would, start their own businesses. Why? China possesses a unique social-political system, a system with only one party and one dominant way of regulating business conduct. So, business success in China to a very large degree depends on knowing how the government works, particularly at the local level where regulations are directly enforced. (A similar situation exists in Eastern Europe.) In China, the old Confucian civil service tradition still lives on—the smartest and the most ruthless go into government. And today the best training for business is a government post!

Why have Mr. Zhu's former students become very successful? Qinghua University has produced more central government officials than any other learning institution. Its graduates hold over 60 of the top 300 Chinese central government posts—those above the vice-ministerial level. Having school-based *guanxi* relationships with these officials greatly benefits the careers of Qinghua MBAs! The old adage proves true: It's not what you know but who you know.

Cowboys instinctively react negatively to this seemingly incestuous relationship. However, a very similar institution exists in the United States; it is called the "revolving door," and it exists primarily within the "military-industrial complex" and other government-regulated industries. In the revolving-door system, the best business leaders get recruited not just into government but into the governmental regulatory bodies that attempt to control the very businesses in which they have worked! Government success depends on knowing how business works: Set a thief to catch a thief. After earning government pensions, these former business leaders then use their connections to get recruited by those same government-regulated businesses to help them once more. Incest is best.

In China, the door typically opens only one way. In America, the door revolves around and around. In each country, connections, or *guanxi,* make the whole thing work. Human nature captured in tradition always wins out over contemporary fads.

DIVERGENT TRADITIONS

The East represents stability over time:

- *Harmony is everything.* The entire universe of gods and men works in harmony. Everything is related, and peace and abundance can only come about through it.
- *Maintaining human harmony* involves the customary rule of the trained scholar-administrator over all other men and women.
- The most important building block of civilization is the *five Confucian-paired relations:* Heaven-earth, Emperor-subject, father-son, husband-wife, and brother-brother. Everyone must become subject to all of these permanent relationships.

- *Family matters far more than the individual.* The individual exists to perpetuate family. There is a concourse of family relations that includes dead ancestors.
- Commercial success comes only through *currying favors* from the rulers.

The West represents dynamic, and sometimes unstable, change:

- *The individual* is the most important element in a civil society. Everything else must yield to individual liberty.
- *Civil society* depends on the impersonal rule of law, not on the rule of men.
- For a civil society to work best, all men and women must be individuals with the *freedom* to think and choose for themselves. The rule of law then polices the dynamic outcomes in a continually changing civil order.
- *All human relationships* have a temporary nature that is always in a state of flux. Nothing is permanent.
- Commercial success comes through hiring *the best and the brightest innovators.*

BUSINESS RECOMMENDATIONS FOR TODAY

1. *Connections.* Business success in China largely depends on connections with local, regional, and central government officials. In America, Cowboys like to keep government out of business dealings whenever possible: Government slows things down and screws things up. Just the opposite holds true in China: Government speeds things up and keeps risks and failures down. Use your Chinese business counterparts' government *guanxi* connections to your advantage.
2. *Advantageous partnerships.* Going it alone in China can be very difficult, if not impossible. The real issue is not *whether* to partner with a Chinese organization but rather *which* organization to partner with. Partners that are well-connected politically can make the difference between success and abject failure.

CASE STUDY

THE JEWISH SYNAGOGUES IN SHANGHAI

During my first trip to Shanghai, an American executive asked me, "Charles, is there a synagogue in Shanghai?" "I'll find out," I told him. That innocent question began a long quest for me. As is the case with most things Chinese, there appears to be no simple answer.

An elderly Jewish woman I know in Florida grew up in China and learned the following story about Jewish origins in that country. It seems that around 800 A.D., a large group of Jewish people from the Middle East, having been driven out by the ruling Moslems, reached Kaifang in Henan Province. They had made the entire, perilous Silk Road journey to escape persecution. The Han welcomed them, and they soon began to settle and intermarry. Some made the journey down the Yangtze River to Shanghai on the seacoast. By now, they looked very Chinese, but they still kept their Jewish beliefs and customs.

Eleven hundred years later, during the Russian Revolution, White Russian Jews also fled and migrated into China. They journeyed to Shanghai, because they learned that a thriving Jewish community existed there. The Russian people, in turn, settled, intermarried and also became absorbed into the broader Chinese culture, still keeping their Jewish beliefs. They came to look Chinese and spoke Hebrew!

I have also learned that Jews from Nazi Germany reached Shanghai before World War II. China was one of the few nations to accept Jews driven from Germany by Hitler's regime. Some also settled in Shanghai, where a vibrant Jewish culture existed. Sadly, under Mao's rule in the late 1940s, the Jews of Shanghai were suppressed—not because of religious beliefs or ethnic persecution but because their institutions appeared to threaten the country's harmony. Today, the government fears the Falun Gong for the same reason.

Please understand that the East does not possess the same dedication to precise historical facts as the West. Some of what I am recounting may not be, in the Western sense, strictly accurate; in China, legend and history readily mix. Nevertheless, Jewish synagogues *have* existed in Shanghai and may do so once more.

I have also heard the story of a Western businessman visiting Shanghai before World War II who asked for a Jewish synagogue. The hotel clerk directed him to one, where he went, only to find himself the sole Caucasian in the place! Everybody else looked Chinese, but every ritual was Jewish. After worship, he approached the

Shanghai Synagogue Web Sites: A number of Web sites pop up on a Google search. Here are a few that you can try:

<www.talesofoldchina.com/shanghai/t-jews.html>
<www.gluckman.com/shanghaijewschina.html>
<www.us-israel.org/source/vjw/chinajews.html>

Rabbi and spoke to him in Hebrew, telling him that he was pleased with the service. The Rabbi expressed his own pleasure, also in Hebrew, at hearing this. Then the businessman said, "By the way, I am a Jew." The Rabbi replied, "Really! You don't look like a Jew!"

Look at what has happened not only for Jews but also for Mongols and Buddhists. First, foreigners immigrated to China either peacefully or by forceful invasion. Then they intermarried and became gradually absorbed by Chinese culture. Finally, they became thoroughly Chinese, while still retaining their ethnic and religious roots. China is not a homogeneous mass; China is a melting pot, although only 5 percent of the total population is non-Han. Furthermore, as the "first America," China became the East's first melting pot some 2,000 years before the United States even existed in anyone's mind.

CHAPTER SIX

Time
WHY EAST AND WEST DIVERGED

DOES TIME TRAVEL IN THE FAST, OR THE SLOW, LANE?

How does time travel? Even to formulate such a question requires Western thinking. Picture a Texan wearing a cowboy hat and driving his pickup truck at 110 miles per hour in the passing lane of an American superhighway with a rifle rack attached to the rear window. Toot-toot goes the Cowboy in his truck, "making time." Get out of my way! The radio blares "Yellow Rose of Texas." Time in the fast lane.

Meanwhile, a Chinese rural peasant pushes a wheelbarrow laden with straw at an agonizingly labored pace over a rough dirt track. The piled straw reaches higher than he does. The wheelbarrow, made largely of wood, has a functional design more than a thousand years old. Time in the slow lane, very slow.

One picture looks very Western, the other Eastern, but the analogy depends on a Western sensibility of time for its meaning. Simply put, in the East, people don't think of time as linear; in the West, we always do. Time is like Route 66.

Is time a straight line, a circle, or perhaps a spiral?

Western linear time goes back to the ancient Hebrews: "In the beginning . . ." If time has a beginning, it also may have an ending, a conclusion that gives a particular urgency to Western life. Cowboys don't even know that most of the world doesn't share their sense for linearly accelerating time that rips them breathlessly along every moment into the future. For the Dragon, time finds its opposite to Western rush and bother: All time is the same.

Time for Love, Anybody?

The grave's a fine and private place,
But none, I think, do there embrace.
—THE ENGLISH METAPHYSICAL POET ANDREW MARVELL

No more potent emotional combination has ever been devised than the Western joining of linear time and human sexuality. Originating with the troubadours of France and Italy in the early Middle Ages, Courtly Love at first explicitly forbade physical union between lovers who were nevertheless in the grip of rushing time. Several hundred years later, sexual union had become the explicit goal, with time representing the constraint. Men became multiple predators—biological psychology at work.

Inevitably, the terminology of hurried and forceful sexual conquest attached itself to business acquisitions. The robber baron business tycoons of the Gilded Age "raped" their weaker competitors and created "forced marriages." The very term *corporate merger* has an obvious sexual connotation; acquisitions get "consummated." In the great takeover decade of the 1980s, "marriages of convenience" occurred, and the threat of corporate rape by the "Louie the Liquidators" of the business world drove companies to seek out "White Knights" for protection. A new age of chivalry was born!

The Chinese have no comparable sense of urgency with regard to time or expressions of time-limited sexuality either. Everything will come to pass in the regular, natural order of things. Predatory business conduct of the raw Western sort violates Confucian harmony. That is not to say that the Chinese lack predatory genes; preying on others in the East is simply done more discretely, using time for advantage rather than perceiving it as a constraint. James Clavell's *Noble House* and the recent brilliant Chinese movie *Crouching Tiger, Hidden Dragon* both illustrate such Eastern predatory conduct. Time is on the Dragon's side, even for the predator.

We may conclude, then, that time interacts with human nature very differently, East and West. One way of thinking about these differences is to consider time working as a cultural catalyst to trigger human interactions with the environment. It is just that the two catalysts have different chemical compositions. Or cultural time has dimensions—like the space-time continuum—but the dimensions happen to be perceived differently. Let's look at cultural time in terms of its dimensions.

THE FOUR DIMENSIONS OF TIME

Cultural time has four dimensions: duration, shape, units, and tense. Let's consider each in turn beginning with *duration*. Most simply, time exists merely as sequential events with no reference to a beginning or an end. Space itself is such a sequence of events—perhaps with an initial Big Bang, perhaps not. Time then becomes merely one of the dimensions to a reality that may be limited to four, or perhaps more that remain undiscovered.

Life, too, may exist as a sequence of events without beginning or end. Birth and death, and perhaps reincarnations, may only represent changes of state, merely sequential events. Or life may have a beginning and an end, an alpha and an omega. Life and time may have existed forever or may be the products of design. Life may be the same from age to age, or it may be evolving.

Is Time a Circle or a Loop?

Does time have *shape?* Strictly speaking, of course, it doesn't, but everyone pictures time in a shape. Traditional agricultural and seafaring communities see time as a circle, as the seasons continually revolve with no real progression. Things stay pretty much the same.

Adherents of the great Western monotheistic religions picture time as a straight line from creation to the end of the world as we know it. Western historians picture time as a great pendulum, in which events swing first toward one extreme, overcorrect themselves, and then swing toward another extreme. Some Western scientists picture time as a wave like those in the ocean; events such as climate change and biochemical processes in the body oscillate like patterns on an oscilloscope. Theoretical physicists may picture time as a ribbon that loops back on itself. Some Western naturalists see events in time moving like a pebble dropped in a pond. This last picture of time is very Eastern.

Time as a circle and time as a line combine to form time as a spiral. A spiral turns continually, but it also goes somewhere. The Irish poet William Yeats wrote of time as a great, turning gyre—that is, the spiraling pathway of a falcon—or the great turning of the universe itself. The image combines the thinking about time and life of both the West and the East. Life can be like the turning of the gyres; our lives either spiral up, or they spiral down. You may choose which direction you want. Upward spirals beat downward ones.

For Cowboys, thinking about time without beginning or end presents great difficulties; Cowboys have become accustomed to starts and stops to the many events in their lives. Thinking about time as a circle or a gyre remains quite alien to most Americans. Cowboys, after all, think of themselves as pretty straightforward people.

Yet all the while Cowboys plunge forward into future time as though on a superhighway stretching across the vast, open plains, a little clock keeps ticking away in memory. Measuring time by the clock doesn't bring the exhilaration of "making time" on the open road; Cowboys have all also learned from the clock a metaphor for life itself ticking away. Cowboys always sense an impending doom.

Want Your Time Whole or in Pieces?

Does time exist in *units* or in unity? Is time discrete or a whole that cannot be divided? Western professionals regard time in the units of their own jargons: Accountants ask if time is a stock or a flow concept; computer scientists question if time works like a digital or an analogue computer; physicists wonder whether time is jerky or smooth; economists are certain that time exists in two states, the short run and long run. To the Western mind, time works like a clock, and it is made up of the ticking hierarchy of seconds, minutes, and hours. Clock time drives the East and West apart.

The West did not always listen to the ticking of the clock. Clock time arrived with the Industrial Revolution, when control over labor shifted from cottage production by individuals to the factory system. Instead of rewarding labor for outputs, labor now got paid by the input—the hours and minutes worked under the supervisor's watchful eye. No such basic change occurred in China.

Time Past and Time Future

Does time possess *tense?* The term comes from the way we categorize verbs within Western languages. Verbs have three simple tenses—past, present, and future—and a number of complex tenses that reveal our personal relationships to time past, present, and future. The tense of time has meaning only with regard to an individual's viewpoint; otherwise, time is merely sequential events. We can only say that time possesses futurity or a past quality, because we stand firmly in the present regarding the events in the string that comprises time itself. Chinese time lacks tense.

In the West, we pinpoint our relationship to that string of events very precisely. Not only that, our complex verb tenses indicate that we regard time as something that we act within forcefully: I *will* have completed my project by tomorrow morning—future perfect, action completed at some precise time in the future. We want to control time, but we also sense it ticking away.

With regard to tense, the most stunning difference between East and West appears immediately when we compare languages: *Chinese verbs have no tense!* Everything gets written and spoken of as though occurring in the present: "I go to the market today; I go to the market yesterday; I go to the market tomorrow." It is all the same. The present and the past coexist, and the future will be pretty much the same, so why bother?

In the East, time is relative; in the West, time is absolute.

We may conclude that what we believe about time determines how time exists culturally for us. Cultural time differs greatly for Cowboys and Dragons (see Figure 6.1), most tellingly in the Western concept of time as a *commodity*, stemming directly from the factory clock. Cowboys literally buy and sell time. They even picture the human mind as a clockworks! For Dragons, time is felt, not thought about.

The West has an overdeveloped head for time and an underdeveloped heart; the East has an overdeveloped heart for time and an underdeveloped head! Somehow, we must learn to meet in the middle.

In the West, time is a commodity that gets bought and sold for its utility value. In the East, time is a leisure good that gets savored and enjoyed.

FIGURE 6.1   How the West and East Regard Cultural Time

The West: Cowboy Time	The East: Dragon Time

1. Truncated time:
   Past, present, future
   Particles that come and go,
     forever?
   Time slots, as at airports
   Clock time
   Present divorced from past and
     future
   Closed-ended, begins and ends
	1. Continuous time:
	   Time flow
	   Movement in circles
	   Temporal merged with eternal
	   Harmonious working
	   Past always present
	   Open-ended, like a river

2. Temporary time:
   Nothing lasts long
   Fractures relationships
   Tears things apart
	2. Eternal time:
	   The great unifier
	   Eternal relationship builder
	   Unifies all things

3. Scientific time:
   Organized and scheduled
   Prompt
   Can be "lost"
   Described by linear or higher-
     level
   Equations
	3. Emotional time:
	   Time is anytime
	   Leisurely and heartfelt
	   Past, present, and future
	     merged
	   Cyclical, continually repeating

4. Thinking about time	4. Feeling about time

5. Time as a commodity:
   Utility value/time value of
     money
   Spend time/save time
	5. Time as a natural process:
	   Value in creating harmony
	   Let time run its course

6. Time as a *business* constraint:
   Time is money
   Profit per quarter
	6. Time as a *business* facilitator:
	   Take time to get it right
	   Make a little for a long time

A BRIEF STORY ABOUT TIME

Differing sensibilities for time can lead to unfortunate international outcomes. The following story illustrates a time conflict within an international business setting, but the situation could just as well be diplomatic. It could even occur as part of arranging a student exchange program. We are simply zoned for different cultural times.

Suppose that an American telecommunications executive—call him Richard Johnson—has been invited to make a follow-up visit to China related to selling advanced electronic switch gear. His Chinese counterpart at the Chinese Ministry of Post and Telecommunications (MPT)—call him Mr. Zhang—wants to acquire such equipment from an American firm. Mr. Johnson's company—call it Millennium Communications Corporation—appears to have an excellent shot at the deal. A first meeting at an American trade show went well; the Beijing visit will go into some depth on the details. Here's what happens:

1. Mr. Johnson arrives in Beijing with slides, viewgraphs, and voluminous handouts in addition to a half dozen sales and engineering experts and two lawyers in tow.

1. Mr. Zhang greets Mr. Johnson with a half dozen colleagues, all of them engineers.

2. Mr. Johnson and his experts give their presentation, recommendation, and justification.

2. Mr. Zhang listens; one of his subordinates takes notes, and nobody asks questions.

3. The American lawyers press for exactitude: "What do you think?" they demand.

3. Mr. Zhang responds: "We'll look into it."

4. The Americans ask for survey data on market size.

4. Mr. Zhang indicates that they will look into it.

Mr. Johnson returns to New Jersey, and his boss asks, "Well, how did it go?" "Fantastic! We'll hear some good news from them in a couple of weeks." A month passes. No news, nothing. Mr. Johnson, feeling heat from his boss, calls Mr. Zhang, who is very polite: "We have been studying your proposal. Some things need clarification. Can you come back?" Mr. Johnson asks if he can fax anything over to speed things up. Mr. Zhang insists on another meeting. The Cowboys return.

In the meeting, Mr. Zhang indicates that things are going well. He has talked to his division head. He also rattles off a number of technical questions that his work unit has regarding the American proposal. Mr. Johnson in turn presses the Chinese for survey data on market size. "We don't know. We have no surveys as such, but we have talked to our colleagues. It is big, very big." Here it is again: the Cowboy habit of breaking things down and the Dragon habit of seeing only a whole. Mr. Zhang goes on to say that the Americans' proposal looks good, but there are still some issues.

Mr. Johnson wonders whether this is a polite rejection. The Cowboys take another tack. They go back over the proposal with their Chinese counterparts and suggest that the Dragons consider a different alternative contained within the proposal. The Cowboys figure that the new alternative will go down better with the Dragons and save some time in negotiating. The reply? "We'll discuss it."

Mr. Johnson returns and tells his eager boss, "This time they're really committed. I think we'll have an answer back in another week." Of course, no response arrives, and more weeks pass. Nearly six months have now gone by since the initial contact. Richard Johnson finds himself losing patience. Another call to Beijing. This time, Mr. Zhang tells him that he is making progress. The proposal has gone up to headquarters, where it is being considered. "Can you come back again? We still need more clarification." How many layers are there? Mr. Johnson wonders. "I'll check with my boss." This time, Mr. Johnson's superior decides to pull the plug on the whole deal.

How many layers are there? It depends on the nature of the project. Sometimes, joint business venture projects have to go to the very top of the People's Republic. *There is no such thing as a discrete business deal in China.* That is Western thinking that cannot apply in a land with very different property ownership. In China, *there is only one owner.*

What went wrong in this deal? Very simply, the Cowboys figured that doing a deal with China should be like doing a deal in Europe or Latin America: proposal, answer objections, close the deal. Time frame: two to four months, beginning to end. Within such an overall scenario, Richard Johnson had a quarterly sales objective to meet, with his bonus hanging in the balance. Don't waste time; get in, close the deal, and get on to the next business opportunity. Each deal represents a discrete business opportunity and challenge. His company's time frame was one business quarter. After all, time is a precious commodity that cannot be wasted. Once a unit of time passes, it is gone forever.

Mr. Zhang, on the other hand, had to consider the well-being of all China. His long-term job prospects and the job prospects of everyone in his work unit hung in the balance. Everything had to be done right, and internal harmony among many related work units had to be assured. Was Richard Johnson a person they could work with over the longer term? Would a supportive relationship be there? As a natural propensity, the Dragons stretch out time: To ensure internal harmony, take some more time to thoroughly discuss things. A business deal, like any other sequence of human events, is a natural process. Let the deal flow along until everything is auspicious and right. Then close the deal; there is no strict time frame. Time is open ended and on our side.

Neither side understood the cultural time sensibility of the other.

GETTING YOUR BUSINESS TIMING RIGHT

Contrast what happened above with the sense of cultural timing that appears in "Cowboy Trying to Be Humble." There, one team of Cowboys had a highly polished presentation and a powerful business proposition. They expected the Dragons to follow Cowboy time, however, and complete a deal within a matter of a few months. They failed—quickly.

The other team committed a number of serious missteps along the way, some of them unavoidable because of the entrepreneurial nature of American industry. They did one thing absolutely right, however; they allowed the entire deal-making process to run on Dragon time, even going so far as flying to Beijing over Christmas. Their deal was consummated, and it lasted.

LESSONS ABOUT CULTURAL TIME
FOR EAST-WEST RELATIONS

- *Clock time versus cultural time.* No matter how loudly or softly the clock ticks, people of different cultures respond to it differently. Cultural time is simply far more complex than any watch.
- *Cowboys and Dragons use business time in inverted sequences.* Cowboys like to develop the deal first, close it quickly, and then work out execution problems as they arise. Relationships develop as the business deal progresses. Dragons like to work out all the issues first, taking a lot of time while ensuring a good relationship. Once the groundwork has been laid, the actual deal can then go forward quickly.
- *Cultural time is emotionally hot for Cowboys and cool for Dragons.* Cowboy time gets chopped up into segments with beginnings and endings, making time blocks into emotional pressure cookers. Cowboy time gets hot emotionally even when it demands cool thinking. Dragon time flows like a river with no sharp borders. It is cool to the senses, a welcoming friend, not an enemy.

RECOMMENDATIONS

1. *Whose turf are you on?* Time runs one way in the East and another in the West. When you go to the East to do business, expect to run on Eastern time, which flows more leisurely but just as purposefully. Neither the trains nor the cultural clock will change schedules just for you! Incidentally, when Dragons seek to do business in the West, they must run on Cowboy time. No excuses!

2. *Know the cultural time zone you are in.* Thoroughly understand the complexities of cultural time for the area of the globe in which you want to do business. This holds for all international business, not just for China and the East.

3. *Disarm cultural time differences.* If you openly discuss your time-related needs *up front,* a middle-course compromise can be reached with the other party. Each party then understands why the other party behaves as it does concerning time. Some flexibility with regard to Cowboy and Dragon time schedules almost always exists.

4. *Rape and pillage.* Dragons have a longstanding fear of predatory Cowboy conduct. Try to push a deal through fast, and you trigger a predation reflex in your counterparts.

CHAPTER SEVEN

Thought
HOW OUR PAST AFFECTS
OUR CHOICES TODAY

Suppose your child has a 102° fever. What will you do? In the West, a mother or father will apply cold compresses to the child's forehead and give the child aspirin. Why? Western parents think about such things from a scientific point of view that counteracts one condition with its opposite. The opposite of hot is cold, so to bring down a fever you apply cold. Basic Newtonian physics.

Wouldn't a Chinese mother do the same thing? A Western parent would think so, but that would be quite wrong. A Chinese mother encountering the very same condition would take the opposite action for a very different reason: She would apply heated blankets to the child! Why? A fever is something in the body that must be sweated out. She only knows that when you apply hot blankets, a fever can almost always be driven out. It has been so for thousands of years; it will be so for many years to come. Native Americans traditionally did the same thing, in a sweat lodge. The Chinese mother possesses an understanding grounded in long experience. A Western scientist would say that her approach is empirical rather than theoretical.

Look what has happened: A Western and an Eastern parent treat exactly the same illness in totally opposite ways, and each treatment works! Neither thought process should be regarded as wrong, even when Western medical science favors one way of thinking. Cowboys and Dragons both might wish to become more cautious in judging how the other side sees reality. Our way might not be the only correct way.

We simply think very differently for reasons related to both our respective traditions and our time sensibilities. The American parents might rush their child to the emergency room; every second is important when

> Sometimes, opposite thinking leads to the same outcome. There is more than one road to truth.

a life is potentially at stake. The Chinese mother trusts that time will work on her side: everything happens, healing included, in a natural manner.

HOW TO "SEE" THE THINKING OF OTHERS

Grasping just how differently people of the West and East think presents a huge challenge for Cowboys and Dragons alike, a challenge that can matter greatly. If you misunderstand how the other side thinks, you may destroy a business or diplomatic opportunity without knowing it.

Much of how we think derives from two sources:

1. How we learn over time
2. What language we use

The first source makes more logical sense than the second: Our teachers help us learn how to think in the terms of our common culture. Language, however, works as another way that our culture passes from one generation to the next: language contains culture, and culture shapes language. So a study of a language also reveals something about how its users think.

> Learning methods and language are the doorways into our invisible thought processes.

HOW WE LEARN

When Learning Begins

The Western parents who have just rushed their one- or two-year-old child to the emergency room don't realize that the child's learning has commenced. The child is too young. Our most common attitude holds that education really begins with kindergarten, or preschool these days. Only limited learning occurs at home; early childhood involves nurturing.

The Chinese regard the family, not the school, as the primary educator of children; formal education merely continues the instruction already begun at home. Also, the Chinese don't consider education to begin at age five or even three. Chinese thinking about when education begins demands an answer to another question first: When does a person's life really begin? For the Chinese, education begins with life, not at a culturally prescribed age.

Cowboys tend to think of *personal* life beginning at birth, because at that moment infants separate from their mothers. Birth marks the point when they begin unique, individual lives. The individual makes up the most important Cowboy entity on earth; everything else should revolve around the "me."

Dragons, on the other hand, believe their lives begin earlier than birth, extending backward to a time even before conception. Such thinking contributes to a Dragon's sense of being a part of the collective, the whole. Birth forms only one, and not the earliest, of life's stages. Because life exists in embryo, a Chinese mother teaches her unborn child. Even the embryonic stage doesn't mark the beginning. The Chinese possess a rich sense for our lives and our learning, all really beginning long ago.

> For Cowboys, life begins at birth; for Dragons, life begins before conception.

Early Collective versus Individual Experience

Chinese beliefs about when life begins help to explain why family, heritage, ancestor worship, and harmonious cooperation matter so much to Dragons. Dragons honor ancestors because they can never really be dead. Within such a world view, Buddhist reincarnation becomes not only possible but natural: I came from, and will return to, this living past. The sum total of all past experience makes up an always present, living strength in each Dragon's existence. I really began 5,000 years ago.

In the West, the closest we get to this sort of thinking comes from the idea of "the collective unconscious" in the psychology of C. J. Jung, who immersed himself deeply in Eastern thought and traditions.

Dragons totally lack the Western sense for private property and privacy. From before birth, they learn about the collective good, not the private domain. Cowboy privacy appears to Dragons as something hidden and negative. Even within the family, privacy has no place. Marriages get arranged by parents, not sworn to in secrecy by lovers. A wealthy family's house in China may have grown to quite a number of rooms, but the rooms don't have a separate hallway for entering them. They are all strung together so that reaching the room at the end means entering and walking through all the rooms before it. After marriage, Cowboys expect their parents to keep some distance away; Chinese parents intrude into their married children's lives in a manner unimaginable in the West. Mothers in the West know what is best for their babies and correct their own mothers; mothers in the East obey their own mother's instructions regarding child rearing.

> In China, parents tell their children how to behave; in America, children tell their parents how to behave.

We may conclude, then, that Cowboys and Dragons from an early age learn to rely on different personal resources—individual versus collective.

> Cowboys say "Trust yourself"; Dragons say "Trust the collective."

Schooling East and West

America has experienced several revolutions in education; China has not. Chinese schooling resembles American schooling before the progressive movement that shaped education to meet children's interests. Our schooling now promotes individual achievement measured broadly as well as personal competition. Chinese education remains authoritarian; the teacher instructs, and the children listen and memorize. Every child is encouraged to excel in school, but competition remains strictly impersonal. Everybody studies the same thing; and examinations define standings just as they did in old China under the emperors.

> Learning looks vertical in China and horizontal in America.

Observing how children play reveals a lot. American parents encourage their children's natural playfulness and also encourage competitive games. Even in team sports, the individual star becomes highly regarded. The Chinese totally lack a sense of play for children; everything in life gets taken very seriously. Children learn how to work, not how to play. Children exercise in groups, and no child is rewarded for excelling in team games. That would breach group harmony.

Life on the Job

Cowboys remain individuals at whatever work they undertake; when an opportunity at another company appears, they quickly jump ship. A job can be fun, and a Cowboy can play at it, enjoying new challenges. Dragons, on the other hand, work as seamless parts of a cooperative work unit, perhaps for a lifetime. Dragons don't play with challenges.

In the West, professional learning gets furthered through the external job market. Professionals search out new job opportunities in the market, shifting jobs and companies frequently and accelerating their exposure to new proprietary skills and knowledge bases and to challenging new career opportunities. Labor markets in the Western sense scarcely exist in China. Work-based learning occurs within the group.

"Discrimination" at Bell Labs

At AT&T in the 1970s, I was the only Asian-American in the entire company doing marketing work. Some Asian-American engineers complained to me about racial discrimination at AT&T: American engineers junior to them in seniority and publications had gotten promotions, and they had not. "Do you get reviewed annually?" I asked them. "Yes." "What is the first thing on the review form?" "Career Objective." "What do you put there?" Their responses were pretty much the same: "I want to be the most distinguished scientist in my discipline."

Bell Labs had two different career ladders: science and management. Managers were promoted; scientists gained distinction. "That's your problem," I told them. "You did not get promoted because you didn't ask to be." The lesson: Training confines; scientific development won't earn promotions. After that, some of the Asian-American engineers opted for management careers; and Asian-American promotions went up at Bell Labs.

FIGURE 7.1   What the West and the East Teach

The West	The East

1. Family education:
    Our baby is a precious, unique individual.
    Give our child the very best.
    Shower an only child with gifts so the child doesn't feel bad.
	1. Family education:
	    All of us are an integral part of the collective.
	    Never have a selfish thought.
	    Remind an only child that the child has cousins.

2. Schooling:
    You are here to learn how to learn, not to memorize.
    The teacher says:
    Question. Learn to have a free spirit. Be creative. Raise your hand when you want to speak.
    "Show and Tell" time tomorrow! Bring something to school and tell about it.
	2. Schooling:
	    Sit together and learn how to write and pronounce this character.
	    The teacher says:
	    Everybody do the same thing. I will assign the responses for you to make.
	    Be obedient! Listen; don't make eye contact with me, just as you don't at home.

3. At work:
    You will get what you want if you work hard and compete successfully.
    Do well enough, and you will get more money and attract a mate.
    You choose your own profession.
	3. At work:
	    You will be assigned a work unit; you have no choices.
	    Your living quarters will be assigned; you will all get paid about the same. Your marriage will be arranged by your family.

How Show and Tell Affects Lifetime Learning

Looking at our lifetime learning differences in Figure 7.1 makes them easy to grasp. Of course, these represent generalizations only; with the advent of market-based reforms and the single-child policy, Chinese education has begun to evidence greater diversity.

The Western "Show and Tell" game highlights the differences between West and East most dramatically. A young Cowboy may bring a frog in a jar to school. During "Show and Tell," when the teacher asks Johnny about the frog, Johnny may reply, "This is a stupid frog!" and then go on to make up a story about the frog that he has named Harry. The story doesn't have to be literally true; in fact, the teacher encourages Johnny to make up a story to use his imagination. In China, such an exercise would never get played. School is for serious learning, so a student "making something up" would be severely punished. "Show and Tell" for Cowboys is more than an innocent childhood game. It initiates a Western child into a world of creativity.

> Show and Tell leads to marketing; strict discipline leads to engineering. In business, many Cowboys become marketers; Dragons are engineers.

Learning Creates Personhood

All of these differences originate in what Cowboys and Dragons have been taught about personhood—individual versus cooperative. Individuated personhood creates the possibility for childhood, school, work, and retirement to exist as distinct life stages. Childhood should be fun; work should be work but with elements of fun as well. After work comes retirement—what Cowboys call "being let out to pasture," a future regarded with mixed emotions.

In retirement, Cowboys believe they should have no responsibilities to others; in return, they lose other purposes in life. In China, grandfatherhood is another kind of work. Dragons regard *all* of life's stages as work. Therefore, there is no humor, as Cowboys know it, in life: Work is serious. Dragons work to gain respect from coworkers, family, and friends.

With individual personhood, friendships become transient in the West; friends may be said to "come and go." Dragons have a word for both friend and "true friend." The Chinese word "true friend" means literally "one who knows me." Cowboys drop one set of friends very opportunistically when another set appears that may benefit them more. Dragons keep friendships for life. One trades; the other accumulates. Cowboys concern themselves with self-knowledge throughout life's stages. They ask: "Am I really like this, or am I changing?" Dragons ask: "Are we like this, or are we changing?"

> Cowboys trade in friendships like cars; Dragons keep friends forever.

These traits and attitudes also affect how each party regards an international business deal, opportunistically versus relationally. Cowboys tend to think in terms of the deal, of how they can make money from it. Dragons tend to think in terms of the trustworthiness of a partner, of how well the two can work together for a long time.

As a result of individualism, the land of the Cowboys has become incredibly diverse. Everyone has been encouraged to adopt a separate identity—racial, ethnic, or gender. In China, just the opposite tradition holds: Individual identity remains a foreign notion. Foreign ideas have always been held at arms' length, if not excluded outright. Relatively few family names exist, because everybody wants a powerful family name association. My own family name—Lee—happens to be among the more common; there are some 90 million Lees in China.

Name Confusion: Cowboy businesspeople often confuse individual Chinese. In part, this is because 19 Chinese family names identify 85 percent of the total 1.3 billion population! No wonder Cowboys think all Chinese are the same.

THE LANGUAGE WE USE

Dragons write sentences vertically, showing a respect for hierarchy. Cowboys write sentences horizontally, showing a sense for journeying across a landscape.

The English and Chinese languages both contain a lot of words, about 400,000 to 500,000 in each case—many more than most languages. (Ancient Hebrew used about 20,000 words; and the modern romance languages contain about one-third the number of words of either English or Chinese.) Both English and Chinese speakers also put about the same number of words into everyday use: 5,000 to 7,000. The similarities end here.

"Hog under a Roof"

The English meaning of "family" derives from the Latin *familia* and means "the members of a household." Family, then, has a fractionalized and logical meaning: those members of a larger social order that belong to the same household—a concept. The Chinese character meaning "family" is formed by drawing the ^ symbol, which means a roof, together with a symbol meaning a hog, that gets placed under the roof. Family in Chinese, then, literally means "hog under a roof." One's family provides the two most important things in life: security and nourishment. The Chinese word for *family* doesn't signify a concept but rather provides an image, a picture of a meaning.

> Cowboy English fractionates whole meaning; Dragon Chinese assembles the pieces of reality into one symbolic whole.

Family has great importance to both cultures, but it means different things. A Cowboy's family can be whoever happens to live together under the same roof. For a Dragon, family means the people and relationships that provide the Dragon with security and nourishment. A Cowboy can divorce and then start a new family—inconceivable in traditional China. Ask both a Cowboy and a Dragon what word they most immediately associate with family. The Cowboy will answer, "children"; the Dragon will answer either "father" or "parents." For one, the family is forward looking; for the other, it is backward looking.

> In China, when you address an envelope, the order for the mailing information is:
>
> - Country
> - City
> - Street
> - Number
> - Person, family name first
>
> This order shows respect for the collective and family over and above the individual.

It becomes easier to grasp the full difference between the English and Chinese languages when the two get compared alongside one another, as shown in Figure 7.2.

FIGURE 7.2   Languages East and West

English	Chinese
1. A language of ideas and concepts Ex: The word *good* expresses a concept.	1. A language of images Ex: *Good* in Chinese is "boy-girl."
2. A language written in symbols having sound meanings—sound bites	2. A language written in stylized picture symbols—visuals
3. Written across the page horizontally	3. Written vertically from top to bottom

4. An exact and precise language using verb tenses and noun genders
    Yes or no
	4. A nebulous language, imprecise in nature and open to multiple meanings
	    Maybe

5. A revolutionary language in which new words get created by individuals Words are entirely new creations. Ex: English word *computer*	5. An evolutionary language created by the collective body New words are combinations of the old. Chinese word *electronic brain,* literally "lightning brain"

"Bright Day Tomorrow"

To see just how conceptual versus imagistic the two languages are, look at their respective words for *tomorrow.* For the West, the next day exists as a temporal period within a linear concept of time itself. English has two words to express this: today and tomorrow. Both words point us toward time just ahead of us. Westerners think about today and tomorrow in terms of discretely divided time. In the Hebrew Bible, God creates in time blocks called "days," showing that this form of thinking goes back very far.

Now consider the Chinese word for *tomorrow.* It begins with the primitive symbol for "man" that looks like a stick man with only a torso and legs (人). Add a horizontal bar at the intersection of the torso line and the legs, and the meaning changes to "big" (大). Add another horizontal bar at the torso's top, and the meaning becomes "sky," or "day"—literally, a man standing under the sky (天). Now put the symbol for "sun" that originally looked like a circle with a dash in the center (the dash indicated that the sun was not a perfect circle) next to a crescent moon with two short strokes inside it. Sun and moon together mean "bright." Put the symbol for "bright" above the symbol for "day," and you have the Chinese word for "tomorrow" (昊)—literally "bright day."

As you know, Chinese has no verb tenses. To sequence things in time, Chinese uses strict grammar rules to avoid confusion: "I work *yesterday;* I work *today;* I work *tomorrow.*" English uses looser structure because it has stricter meaning. The same holds true for expressing mood in the two languages.

The Chinese word for *tomorrow* describes the whole image of a person viewing the newly risen, bright sun. The sunrise itself has no reference to the passing of one day and creation of the next day; all days are pretty much the same. Western words accommodate the idea of the Platonic ideal form; Chinese words recognize only the concrete, pictorial sensibility for reality. In these regards, language has both shaped and been formed by very different thought processes.

English has the gender words *he, she,* and *it.* Chinese has one word, *ta,* that means "he," "she," or "it"! Gender is either implied (by a name) or specified.

Doing Business: What Gets Lost in Translation

Poetry is what gets lost in translation.
— ROBERT FROST

Cowboy-Dragon differences come together with potentially devastating effect when the two parties sit down to formulate a written agreement. The critical question will inevitably arise: In which language shall we write the agreement? The fair thing almost always seems to be to write it in both languages. Usually, this means first writing it into English, which, after all, is a language rich in contractual terminology. Then the agreement gets translated from English into Chinese. The Cowboy lawyers now have what they want—a tight, logical legal document. The Dragons feel they have accommodated the Americans, and they have the protection of a contract written in Chinese. No one expects conflict over the meaning of the contract, which inevitably will arise. Both sides will feel betrayed when challenged about a document that is "the same" in both languages. What has happened?

The answer appears in the relative degrees of precision in the two languages. The initial translation from English to Chinese demanded that the translator choose among several different, and sometimes subtle, permutations of meaning existing within the Chinese language. When another Chinese translates the contract back into English, another set of choices among translation permutations has to be made because each Chinese expression admits of several more narrow English versions. By the time the second English version emerges, the Americans become outraged by the Chinese "treachery." Because English doesn't convey the subtleties of Chinese, allowing the Chinese document to contain *one* sense of the English original, the reverse translation may force out the intended meaning and introduce an unintended meaning on a take-it-as-is basis. Not only poetry gets lost in translation.

> Confused translation allowed Americans to interpret the 2001 "spy plane" letter of "apology" as expressing "regret," while permitting the Chinese to translate it into an abject apology for a wrong action.

Even simple conversation can trip up Cowboys and Dragons. Consider how Chinese "measure words" confuse Americans. Every Chinese noun has a measure word that goes with it as a part of speech rather than as a strict quantity limit. For instance, the measure word going with chopsticks is *one* pair; the Chinese ask for one pair of chopsticks the way Americans ask for *some* silverware. Americans often take Chinese measure words literally, so a Cowboy developer, for example, might ask about the air-conditioning for a new hotel. His Chinese partner may reply, "Oh yes, one air conditioner." "No," screams the Cowboy, "air-conditioning in every room!"

> Cowboys seek intellectual understanding: a meeting of the minds. Dragons seek emotional understanding: a meeting of the heart.

What Is the Issue?

When such misunderstandings arise—and they almost inevitably do—everybody naturally tends to define the problem in terms of who is wrong and who is right. That is wrong. The issue must never become who is right but rather who knows whom better in a positive and benign sense. This kind of knowing comes from emotional understanding, a holistic matter, not merely intellectual understanding. When both Cowboys and Dragons learn more about who the other actually is with regard to tradition, time frames, and thinking, translation difficulties and problems understanding the other side's thinking will recede into the background.

> Knowledge of the other makes up the secret competitive advantage in international business.

THINKING ABOUT OUR DIFFERENCES

- *Theoretical and empirical.* Western theoretical thinking doesn't automatically trump Eastern empirical thinking. Each can get you to a good outcome.
- *The depth of our differences.* Cowboys and Dragons learned to think differently long before birth. Learning traditions and language itself assure this. We cannot change it, but we can disarm some otherwise fatal consequences if we recognize it.
- *The secret competitive advantage in international affairs.* When we thoroughly know the other party, we gain the most powerful competitive advantage possible. Knowing the other party means knowing that party's traditions, beliefs, sensibilities about time, and habits of thought. Then we can become friends rather than adversaries.

A FEW THOUGHTFUL RECOMMENDATIONS

1. *Let go of rationality hang-ups.* Don't be overly concerned how your counterparts have thought through a decision. Accept the result. Chances are, you won't understand their process anyhow!

2. *Eliminate translation confusion.* Share translators who are *bicultural* as well as *bilingual.* This goes against Cowboy sensibilities governing conflicts of interest, but it works best.

3. *Forget about adversarial relations.* Let go of the Cowboy notion that your relationship with the other party has to be a legal, adversarial one symbolized by squads of lawyers and separate translating teams.

4. *Use the secret competitive advantage.* When you know your counterparts thoroughly, most sources for confusion and conflict largely disappear. Translation problems get minimized because you already know what the other side really means.

CHAPTER EIGHT

Transitions
WESTERN AND EASTERN
WORLDS IN FLUX

Everything that I have told you so far about how Dragons think, feel, and behave today may be wrong! Following the Communist and Cultural Revolutions (1949 and 1967–1976, respectively), China entered into a revolutionary period that has seen traditional attitudes replaced, first by Maoist pressures and then by marketplace "reforms." Today in China, many younger people, especially in coastal enterprise areas (see Figure 8.1), no longer receive guidance from their parents. Instead, they have become marketplace oriented, resembling young Cowboys in America!

A Word of Caution: No matter what age, a Dragon is still *Chinese*—not a Westerner.

CHANGES IN DRAGON TRADITION AND THEIR EFFECT

The great modern Chinese migration from countryside to city has created a huge, sometimes homeless, migratory population. Many new urban workers come from traditional peasant backgrounds but find themselves thrust into something close to a transient Western environment. In the Chinese enterprise zones, traditional rules no longer hold. A current best-seller in China aims to teach good manners to an increasingly unruly, urban Chinese population.

Changes in many traditional rules make understanding Dragons much more difficult for Cowboys. Some Chinese remain completely traditional, following Confucian social rules. Other Dragons have become

FIGURE 8.1   A Population Distribution for China in Transition

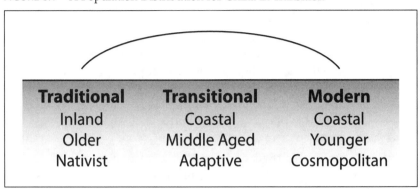

Traditional	**Transitional**	**Modern**
Inland	Coastal	Coastal
Older	Middle Aged	Younger
Nativist	Adaptive	Cosmopolitan

News Flash! A recent *Wall Street Journal* article mentions that newly created wealth in China has led to a "grave craze." Under Mao, the government had suppressed the tradition of building elaborate tombs for ancestors. Now that has all changed, and some Chinese build posh modern mausoleums for themselves—while they are still alive.

more like amphibians—both traditional and modern in their outlooks and often vacillating between the two. The safest course for Cowboys? Assume that your Dragon counterparts still hold traditional values until they signal otherwise.

If Cowboys are like eagles, Dragons are becoming more and more like amphibians.

REVOLUTIONS NEW AND OLD

Revolutionary changes have been very important over time in both the East and West. However, when we look into the matter of revolutions, we quickly find that they have come in two forms: traditional and modern. Chinese history evidences a number of traditional revolutions but only a few modern ones. The West has experienced a number of modern revolutions but relatively few traditional ones. The difference is more than semantic.

The word *revolution* itself refers to the action of something turning or rotating in a full circle, as in the orbital motion of celestial bodies. In this sense of the word, a revolution in human affairs only brings things back to where they had been before some force spun them around.

The Chinese Empire experienced many revolutions that involved the overthrow of dynasties that had become too oppressive and had upset the traditional relations between government and governed. After a period of turmoil, things came full circle, and a new family reestablished traditional rule under the Mandate of Heaven. A number of times an imperial decree ended Chinese foreign exploration and trade; similar restrictions on internal growth and development also occurred. Merchant and military class aspirations often received severe setbacks. Why did these traditional sorts of revolutions occur in China? They protected the harmony of interests that held the empire together.

Harmony can be as costly as conflict. Harmony cost China its world leadership in technology.

The West of course has also experienced such traditional revolutions, as recently as 1848, the Year of Revolutions in Europe—nearly all of them overthrown by traditional forces. Traditional revolutions in the West, however, pale in significance compared with the West's modern sort. Modern Western revolutions caused the civilizations of Europe to overtake the Chinese Empire in economic activity and innovation in roughly the 16th century. Progress doesn't lie in going around in circles.

The modern sense of revolution has nothing to do with the word's original meaning. Modern revolution involves a complete alteration of affairs—no going back. Traditional revolutions, of course, meant the same old thing all over again. New revolutions have meant a good deal of upheaval—even occasionally something to lose one's head over, as in France during the Reign of Terror.

The old sort of revolution found change pretty revolting; the new sort finds revolt pretty entertaining.

The first modern political revolution in China took place in the third century B.C. and created the imperial system of government. That system lasted until 1911—at least in part because its omnipresent demand for harmony allowed no challenges. The corresponding, and nearly contemporary, modern revolution in the West established the Roman Empire and *Pax Romana*. Even before that, another Western revolution had created the Greek city-state. Political revolution in the West didn't end here. The follow-up to Rome began in the Middle Ages and yielded the modern nation-state. The modern Western revolutions that followed really explain the obvious: Cowboys and Dragons are very different animals.

ALL IN THE FAMILY

The next modern Western upheavals began with the 14th-century Commercial Revolution. Venice in particular saw its merchant traders generate vast new wealth from international dealings in fine Venetian cloth and glassware. That new wealth required two sorts of new skills: innovative manufacturing and trading techniques. It turned out that Venetian artisan's skills remained generally inferior to those of China. The new trading techniques, however, had far greater future consequence. These new practices developed out of an old need.

In both West and East, private economic activities, whether in agriculture or trade, had always been carried out by family concerns. Every paterfamilias knew that you could be far more certain of the honesty of family members than of other folk, if only because you could more easily discipline errant sons. Nothing would have changed, East or West, if the Venetians hadn't grown their businesses too fast and run short of viable family members. My kingdom for more sons.

To this day, the Chinese greatly prefer to organize private enterprise along family lines, whereas the West fancies the faceless corporation. Even outside mainland China, in such places as Malaysia and Indonesia, Chinese expatriates run rather large enterprises strictly under family management. Some younger members go off to study at the Harvard Business School, which produces some highly interesting family tensions when they return.

Regarding successful large Chinese family-run businesses, you may wish to look at *Inside Chinese Business* by Harvard Business School Professor CHEN Ming-Jer.

Not having enough family to go around, the great Venetian and other Italian family merchant houses found alternative ways to ensure trust within the business services provided by their employed agents, both at home and overseas. A major part of the solution took the form of what we now know as double-entry bookkeeping—a revolution in the means for stopping thieves. Heretofore, the idea had been to prevent theft before it occurred by using family members who, being more trustworthy, were less likely to steal in the first place. Now the theft solution took the form of making it harder to hide business frauds. And, despite the recent flap over accounting scandals, it still works today.

Western merchants using nonfamily agents also needed to be quite precise about their private property rights and about just who had the authority to do what and for how much. Modern contract law and private property rights, along with enforcement mechanisms, began to develop about the same time. All of these finally-tuned techniques, refined over some seven centuries, have recently come as quite a shock to Dragons, who all along had gotten by with family firms and informal property arrangements.

The flip side of trust arises as security—or rather, insecurity. In a perfectly secure world, trust is irrelevant. In a very insecure world—such as southern and western Europe in the Middle Ages—provision for security of property extended beyond the normal need for trusted services within the counting house to security of property in transit. Double-entry bookkeeping could not protect gold shipments from thieves.

So the Italians invented the bill of exchange—a written, negotiable, and discountable instrument of trade requiring the addressee to pay the bearer on demand. Relatively safe and cheap to administer, bills of exchange rapidly replaced bullion payments for most international transactions. Discountable, they created the basis for the world's first international banking system. In China, meanwhile, security for gold shipments never amounted to a big problem because of the internal harmony of the empire achieved through enlightened administration.

The handwritten bill of exchange of the West changed the world more than did the Chinese invention of printed paper money. The instincts behind the two inventions differed; Dragon paper money expanded several art forms—paper making, artistic design, ink making, and printing itself. Paper money promoted harmony within the realm by eliminating hard money shortages and facilitating internal trade. Its value stopped at the empire's borders, which is the way the Emperors wanted it. The Western bill of exchange, far cruder physically, set off an explosion in sophisticated financial instruments down to the complex derivatives of our present time. Whether the rulers of the petty fiefdoms of the West desired that or not did not matter; they could not stop it.

> The Chinese Emperor ordered the creation of paper money to facilitate tax collection; Western nation-states facilitated paper credits to create more trade transactions.

PAYING BY THE CLOCK

The next great modern revolution in the West had even larger effects; its "dark, satanic mills" had begun to turn full speed by the mid-18th century in Great Britain. Two things about the Industrial Revolution clearly matter in comparing the West with China: clock time and machinery.

The Industrial Revolution's great entrepreneurs saw early on that recompensing workers for their outputs would never make capital investments pay: Workers remained in control of their time and could set the work pace that pleased them. On the other hand, when workers contracted with entrepreneurs to sell their time, labor could become far more efficient, especially when given generous amounts of capital equipment. The foreman's discipline saw to that. Labor-saving capital quickly produced biblically proportioned 100-fold increases over the old, labor-intensive methods. The great time clocks in the old factory towers still tell the tale.

Machinery and the Reserve Army

Karl Marx observed the legions of men and women displaced from traditional handicraft pursuits by the "machine," and from his table in the British Library he named them the Reserve Army of the Unemployed. The Dragons of the Far East also observed the wrenching reallocations of people's lives in the West. They shuddered and rejoiced that the Chinese system produced no such harsh results.

> Even today in China, Dragons will point to the Industrial Revolution's harmful effects on workers' lives as a condemnation of capitalism and a confirmation of China's superiority.

If Cowboy entrepreneurs have always had a fascination with machine-driven efficiency, the Mandarin Dragons of China have remained deeply resistant to it. One wishes to make short work of anything; the other prolongs work so that everybody may have work to do. Under the Mandate of Heaven, the Emperors had always concerned themselves with two things: that the people had enough to eat and enough work to do. If a machine, such as a canal lock for raising boats upstream, could contribute to the public well-being, all well and good. Let such inventions go forward. If a hand tool, such as a new type of wheelbarrow, could help a peasant feed his family, so much the better.

The Dragons didn't even conceive of machines replacing men, however. Through the workings of harmony, the ruling Dragons could systematically deny private profit opportunities for the merchant class who might otherwise be expected to use Chinese ingenuity to develop labor-enhancing equipment. The entrepreneurs of the West did have such opportunities, with revolutionary results.

WEST OVERTAKES EAST

Does the Industrial Revolution, then, account for why the Cowboys of the West caught up to, and then surpassed, Chinese economic capabilities? By no means. Western Europe overtook China economically *before* the Industrial Revolution began. To better understand why China was overtaken by the West, we need to look at how the Chinese social order, compared to the West, treated gains from productive employment prior to its modern revolution of 1949. Who won out before the People's Revolution?

First of all, as a principle of human conduct, the more capable individuals in any society tend to pursue careers that promise them the highest economic returns. Today, when well-educated Chinese-Americans recognize that greater economic returns in Cowboy land come from management and marketing, and entrepreneurship, many of them become managers and marketers, and some start their own companies. Back in China, most of these people would have become engineers—whether they wished to or not. No unique Cowboy gene, or genius, exists for entrepreneurship.

In the old Chinese Empire, the returns from private entrepreneurship appeared rather meager. Harmony demanded that no individual or family should reap large gains in trade in violation of Confucian principles, or threaten to put neighbors out of work. An administrative hierarchy

Today, Silicon Valley entrepreneurs from the Far East have become so common that they are called "ICs"—short not for integrated circuits but for "Indian-Chinese"!

that extended downward from the Emperor to the local village ensured that correct relationships between people were followed—including prohibitions against profit taking by the lowly merchant class. Government officials extracted business profits in the form of politely forced "gifts," with a share going to each official's superior until gifts reached the top. In the profit game, the Emperor won.

Of course, at any one time, only so many administrative plums grew on the government tree. The competition via national examinations for these civil service appointments grew very intense: Enlightened administration offered the greatest economic and social rewards to the most enterprising and talented Dragons. Gifts to officials higher up the hierarchy bought the rental of rights to profit from tax collections and fees for government services. Dragons competed for the administrative plums.

What Dragons call "gifts" even to this day, Westerners call "bribes."

In the West, meanwhile, a revolution in thinking gave to a man the fruits of his own labors. Profits went to private enterprise. China fell behind the nations of the West precisely because the harmony system encouraged public rent–seeking behaviors and discouraged private profit–seeking behaviors among the country's most talented individuals and families. In the West, the world turned upside down; in the East, things remained the same.

MODERN REVOLUTION COMES TO CHINA

Modern revolutionary forces in the West created a nearly continual state of social transition, beginning in the late Middle Ages and lasting to the present. Cowboys remain transitional figures riding through an ever-changing, technology-rich landscape. China remained insulated from such forces for a very long time—until 1949. Then, Mao's triumph set off modern revolutionary actions aimed at breaking a 2,200-year-old stagnation. China has been in transition ever since.

The Communist Revolution in China appeared very threatening to Cowboys at the time. Political revolution itself frightened Westerners, who had grown used to peacefully voting governments out of power (especially in Italy). The West forgot that China, always under dynastic rule, had no other way to change its government except by revolution. In China, revolutions happen when things grow desperate enough for the common men and women.

Cowboys have always emphasized the *communist* part of China—*godless* communism no less. American scholars wondered endlessly after 1949 about why the Chinese people embraced an ideology so alien to their traditions as communism, which, after all, was thought out in the British Library in the mid-19th century by a German immigrant who failed at everything else in life. The simple truth somehow escaped them: The revolution of 1949 involved an attempt to change the nation's inherited *culture*, not its *ideological beliefs*. The Chinese not-so-secret mantra regarding authority has always been: Believe what you want, so long as you rule us at a distance, and don't steal too much from us.

> Cowboys believe that Americans are unique in their desires for limited government. In reality, the Dragon gentry and peasants of China have sought limited, and very distant, government for thousands of years.

After the revolution, Cowboys assumed that the newly developed Chinese aggressiveness toward the West meant that China wanted to join the now-defunct Soviet Union in creating the single workshop of the world, a communist nightmare utopia. In reality, the new ruling Dragons merely wanted to dispel Western invaders and regain national pride and ascendancy—*and* revitalize a moribund economy.

The West simply backed the wrong horse in the form of the Kuomintang (KMT), or Nationalist Party. Its leader, CHIANG Kai-shek, attempted to rule in the old way of all the emperors, and failed. The revolution that ultimately brought him to power was merely another in a long line of old-style ones that sought to return to the traditional status quo power relationships. The revolution brought on by MAO Tse-tung had quite a different nature, one that few Cowboys understand.

The Kuomintang "lost" China the same way numerous other ruling parties had lost dynastic control—forfeiting the people's trust and confi-

> The Communist Revolution was not about ideology, except on the surface; it was about changing culture and basic social arrangements.

dence by, in turn, greedily extracting too much wealth from them. Mr. Chiang himself behaved as though he owned China, and the Chinese people were his "children." The Communist Party "won" China by engaging with the Chinese people at the local level and so regaining trust, something truly revolutionary.

COME THE REVOLUTION . . .

Women hold up half the Heavens.
—A CHINESE APHORISM

Chairman Mao faced a unique dilemma. The old Emperors had erected a structure stronger than perhaps anyone ever knew. As a result, China seemed *culturally* incapable of adapting to either modernizing social forces or scientifically and technologically driven economic development. The big stumbling blocks to any change appeared to be the twin cultural pillars: Emperor Rule and Confucianism.

A number of great leaders successfully led modern revolutions because they correctly identified one or two things that needed to change—and then changed them. During the Great Depression, the Roosevelt Administration focused on two things: stabilizing the banking system and inflating prices, with about a 50 percent success rate. Chairman Mao focused on destroying Confucian hierarchical harmony and the exclusive rule of kinship relations, also with limited success. Maoist reforms did greatly improve the lot of Chinese women. His techniques did not often appear very nice to the West, but then, the obstacles to success also appeared huge.

> The teachings of Chairman Mao didn't purpose to indoctrinate Dragons into Communist ideology; they attempted to replace Confucian principles with more egalitarian ones.

Westerners soon belittled the "Great Leap Forward" that saw peasants trying to make steel in backyard furnaces, sensing that it was a bit like the Israelites trying to make bricks without straw. As a purely economic plan, it failed miserably, but its goals never had been purely economic or measurable in terms of annual GDP. The Great Leap Forward aimed at further breaking down the traditional peasant family's father-dominated role in Chinese society. It sought to create a revolution across the psycho-social landscape far more than across the economic one. To some degree, it succeeded.

To break patriarchal kinship rule, Mao encouraged women's equality, which led to *asexual* roles everywhere, including business and diplomacy.

The great Cultural Revolution that followed in China can be seen as the Emperor Mao's frustrated response to peasant intransigence and to continued kinship dominance of social arrangements. The Cultural Revolution in China arose in the 1960s, approximately concurrent with the Sexual Revolution in the West, especially in America.

You may wish to look at Francis K. Hsu's *Americans and Chinese: Passages to Differences* for a more thorough understanding of all these changes.

REVOLUTION—SIXTIES STYLE

Social revolutions in the West—such as labor and prohibition movements, and populist farm movements—have never come from direct government action. They have been the spontaneous result of voluntary action groups. The Sexual Revolution in America held to this tradition, being driven first by political, antiwar activists and then by feminist groups. The Cultural Revolution in China was instigated and directed by Chairman Mao himself; it constituted a government-led revolution against private social institutions, rather than the other way around as in the West.

The Cultural Revolution in China became possible through a revolutionary change in the goals of a centralized, hierarchical government descending from the rule of a single personality. The Sexual Revolution

> Western social revolutions come from private groups; Chinese social revolutions come from government.

stemmed from *technology,* following other 20th-century revolutions in how we work with, and relate to, one another—facilitated by improved household and communications technology. Group work relations, especially between men and women, have throughout history been determined by how work can best get done—that is, by technology. The Pill has been in this regard one of the latest, and most profound, social change agents in human history—right up there with sedentary agriculture and gunpowder.

> Much of what the Chinese find offensive about America comes from its Sexual Revolution, whose effects are beginning to change China too.

China missed these technological revolutions because of its change-resistant social system. Chairman Mao didn't intend the Cultural Revolution to enable China to catch up with the West technologically but rather to create an improved, centrally controlled, and professionally administered new Chinese Empire. So both the sources and goals for these great sixties' revolutions appear very different.

THE AFTERMATH

[We are] crossing the river by feeling the stones.
— DENG XIAO PING

When the excesses of the Cultural Revolution became apparent, and Mao died, another revolution, a very traditional one, occurred in China, replacing in 1978 the rule by the Gang of Four who followed Mao dynastically with yet another emperor figure. DENG Xiao Ping surprised everyone by leading China cautiously into market-based incentives for remaking an economy ravaged by the Cultural Revolution. Collective farming got replaced by "the household responsibility system"—something curiously like the old kinship principle. China had patiently out-lasted Mao's reforms.

Mr. Deng allowed cash crops and informal markets to flourish at a pre-viously unheard of level of market-based initiative in the previously tightly regulated Chinese economy. Unsurprisingly, the economy re-sponded with the largest annual growth rates in the world. Rural Chinese living in poverty declined by a quarter from 1978 to 1984. China became one nation with two economies, a traditional one of state monopolies and another of private enterprises—bureaucrats and businesspeople.

Private enterprise linked to foreign investment has challenged the tra-ditions of Old China more strongly than Mao's reforms could have ever done. Perhaps the marketplace will do what the Cultural Revolution could not—permanently change the family-kinship pillar of Chinese society. All of this explains why much of what I have told you may no longer be true: the old traditions have been threatened more by the mar-ketplace than by the thought of Chairman Mao.

While Chairman Deng encouraged gradual reforms, the Cowboys of America created another technologically driven, radical new revolution: the Internet, the new virtual global communications superhighway for the future. The Internet has changed forever the way Cowboys work and play and will have totally unpredictable consequences as well for Drag-ons. The combination of market reforms and global communications places China, too, into a new era of transition.

WHERE ARE WE ALL GOING?

An exciting, or perhaps frightening, thing about transitions is that we cannot know where they will end up. Three possibilities appear to exist for both the Cowboys and the Dragons: One, we earthlings may have entered into a permanent state of continuously changing social arrange-ments, one with no apparent end and in which transition becomes perma-nent. Two, we may be entering into a completely new and stable *global* social arrangement unlike any that has existed before. Or three, we may be absorbing current changes while on a pathway back to social arrange-ments still based in our respective traditions, East and West. No one can say with any certainty where the current flux of change will lead, but I believe that the third way will prove to be the new reality. If so, East and West will remain substantially different, still like two different worlds, but we will have learned more about each other in the process.

SOME REVOLUTIONARY CONCLUSIONS

- *Technological preeminence.* China lost technological and economic preeminence to the West because the emperors created a system in which the gains from government positions exceeded the gains from private enterprise. The best and the brightest went into government.
- *The Communist Revolution* was not about ideology or world conquest; it was about creating a more *egalitarian* society within China.
- *The revolutions that have mattered most* in the world have been driven by *technology*, not by politics.
- *China is currently in transition.* Nobody can say for sure where the transition will lead, but it almost certainly won't make the Chinese just like us. Expect that Cowboys and Dragons both will experience positive changes, but that in the end we will remain dominated by our own traditions.

RECOMMENDATIONS

1. *Don't* engage your Chinese counterparts in ideological warfare! You may think you will win an argument, but you will lose at international business.
2. *Do* learn enough about the real nature of China's revolutionary past to engage in polite questioning about it.
3. *Do* be prepared to give a reasonable explanation for how the long-term gains from the Industrial Revolution have overshadowed its negative short-term consequences a long time ago. Explain to your counterparts that the harms were once great, but that period is now past.

PART THREE

Beliefs: The Core of Business Practices

Business life is about "bringing home the bacon"—or is it more like a home away from home? More is always better than less—or is it? Nice guys finish last—or do they? The Law is The Law—or is it? Every one of these cherished Western clichés may hold true for us, but nothing works the way you'd expect in the Middle Kingdom between Heaven and the nether regions. It is as though you have moved to a world where all the laws of physics have become inverted. Stuff falls up.

West and East begin with very different philosophies about such basics as money and banking, private versus social gains, investment, the virtues of competition, and the rule of law. You can learn about the differences now, or you can learn the hard way in real life.

CHAPTER NINE

Philosophies
HOW EAST AND WEST VIEW BUSINESS

It's love without marriage.
—A WESTERN MERGER AND ACQUISITION EXPRESSION

I can do anything I want, so long as I don't attract attention.
—A CHINESE BUSINESS EXPRESSION

TWO METAPHORS FOR DOING BUSINESS

Single metaphors dominate business talk, East and West. It's sex for the Cowboys along with its suggestions of power gained over others. For Dragons, it is family, understood broadly to include even the state. Sex and family obviously have an intimate relationship but not the way Cowboys and Dragons use them. Neither brings sex and family together, metaphorically speaking. Cowboy sex-speak is bluntly direct; Dragon family-speak is oblique.

Cowboys view business as linear and direct; Dragons view business as circular and indirect.

Business Like Love without Marriage

Sexual metaphors dominate everyday Cowboy business language, much as sexual innuendo dominates Shakespeare. In each, a whole range of sexually oriented metaphors prevails—such as rape, whoring, infidelity, and marriage of convenience. A takeover artist may seek to rape and pillage company coffers; an industry may be a "whore's market." Even at the personal level in business, the sexual prevails: Cowboys speak of "sticking it" to someone.

In the direct, linear West:
Man loves woman for sex,
Woman gives man sex for love.

In the indirect, circular East:
Man marries as a family obligation;
Woman enters man's world.
Number One obligation is to produce a male heir.
Flower (or Geisha in Japan) world exists for erotic outlets.

A Cowboy does business the way he makes love: for conquest. A Dragon does business the way he relates to his extended family: for respect.

Business Like Family Relations

The pig is afraid to get fat, and the wise man is afraid to be smart.
—AN OLD CHINESE SAYING

In traditional China, the grandfather manages the family and its financial affairs—and makes the most money. The government bank that "gives" out money from the "kitty" to deserving "sons" gets called the "grandfather." A family business aims to earn the family respect, not necessarily to grow bigger. Earning the family respect means serving customers in a local village or neighborhood. Growing too big violates the family's hierarchy of place and the harmony of the local social order. Also, growing too big could threaten the family's livelihood—someone in the government hierarchy might then wish to "help" the business. Beware of too-powerful "uncles" in government.

None of this means that Chinese businesses are not entrepreneurial or very competitive; it simply means that the context for competition differs greatly from the American one. A family business in China cannot gain a customer until a family member first establishes a relationship with a person. That means taking ritualistic, subservient positions with each potential customer. The businessperson appears low down in the social hierarchy and must continually signal his lowliness to win and keep customers. Chinese businesspeople compete vigorously in this ritualistic manner.

> Cowboys perform impersonal marketing to "consumers"; Dragons perform personal selling to "customers."

Someone in the authoritarian hierarchy, traditionally the emperor, can expropriate a private business. The law's impact locally depends on how a government official interprets it. The behavior of Dragon businesspeople gets determined by both the social custom requiring subservience and the need to avoid the attention of government officials. Dragon businesspeople act like women avoiding the advances of predatory males.

Cowboy businessmen are hemmed in by generally enforced laws, and they adapt their behavior to avoid lawsuits. Their Dragon counterparts enjoy nearly complete freedom from legal requirements so long as they don't alarm government officials. Who is more free?

The closest analogy to Chinese business practices in the West appears within the ethnic family business traditions still present among certain nationalities. Some ethnic groups have brought these traditions to America. In some instances, family businesses in China may take on elements of Mafia behavior in their competitive responses to one another, but customers in China still receive subservient respect. Both countries have their Mafia ways.

THE MONEY TRAIL

All money belongs to the Emperor.
—AN OLD CHINESE ADAGE

The money supply is too important to trust to government.
—MILTON FRIEDMAN

East and West invented money at about the same time, but each uses money very differently. In China, the government traditionally supplied money to make it easy to collect taxes; in the West, governments eventually supplied money to further business transactions. In both cultures, banks play an important role in creating the money supply. There the similarities largely end.

Western banks work as stand-alone, profit-seeking enterprises; they help create the money supply as an unintended consequence of private lending. Many years ago, Western banks used to loan out money on the basis of a borrower's character, but that no longer obtains. Banks now lend money based on the basis of *creditworthiness*, not *personal worthiness*. They lend money based on the risk-weighted likelihood that loans will be repaid at a profit to them. They lend money on the basis of financial statements; and when the risk appears too high, they won't lend money at all. Then, different institutions come into play, such as the Cowboy-created venture capital firm. Everything relates to risk-reward assessments.

> Cowboys lend money on the basis of creditworthiness; Dragons lend money on the basis of personal worthiness.

All Chinese banks belong to the government. They both take in and lend out money to further social purposes. Profit-related risk-reward calculations simply do not get made, at least not until very recently. No avowedly risk-seeking financial institutions existed in China until very recently either, when a fledgling venture capital effort began. I know, because I helped start it.

When a Chinese company gets into financial trouble, a government bank feels obligated to lend it more money to preserve the work unit and social harmony. A Cowboy company, of course, will see its borrowing capabilities disappear and its shareholders dump its stock. Hardly any businesses went bankrupt in China until recently, but many do in the West.

Even today, a Dragon entrepreneur approaches a bank for a loan not on the basis of an attractive business opportunity but rather on the basis of being a deserving person from a respected family. The "grandfather" banker may then give the businessperson money from the "kitty." Lending still doesn't stem from the profit potential of the business calculated as a return against clock time: The time value of money doesn't exist. Instead, the social harmony value of money determines who will receive it. The recipient may spend at least part of it on what Cowboys regard as illegal personal uses. For the Dragon businessperson, however, such uses cement relationships within the broader social harmony. What can earn you a jail term in the West possesses perfect legitimacy in the East.

> Cowboys think of the time value of money; Dragons regard the social value of money.

NONPROFIT SECTORS

Large business enterprises do, of course, exist in China, alongside millions of small family-centered ones. The State owns all the large monopolies that have no direct competitors. The Emperor used to own everything; today, the State does.

In some ways, the Chinese large business sector resembles the American nonprofit sector. In each case, nothing resembling a Profit and Loss Statement (P&L) exists. Investment and working capital gets allocated through budgets, not through profitable performance. State-owned banks work somewhat like large United Way charitable organizations, although they don't, strictly speaking, raise donations. They do allocate money based on social priorities rather than on business ones. Loss-making enterprises can and do continue on for years while smaller, private firms may starve for capital: The social consequences of bankruptcy would not be acceptable. While people in the West consider such practices reprehensible, the Chinese regard them as normal. After all, emperor-owned monopolies have a 2,000-year-old history.

The United Way scandal outraged many Americans: executives building personally controlled empires and living off huge expense accounts while remaining unaccountable to the people who donated money to help the disadvantaged and the poor. The same behaviors occur in China's state-owned monopolies, but there they are tolerated. When Western journalists act outraged by these behaviors, the Chinese point their fingers to the West's "outrageous" executive salaries and bonuses, particularly in America. Enron has not helped the U.S. reputation. Chinese salaries remain small and get determined by social position, not by individual performance. To the Chinese, American executives are walking embodiments of greed.

CATEGORIES FOR OUR DIFFERENCES

Our business differences fall into three categories: (1) outlooks on gains from business dealings, (2) relationships between business firms, and (3) rules of business conduct. What we Cowboys regard as good, healthy profits, our Dragon counterparts see as active greed. Cowboys value individual and corporate competition as a means of bringing out the best in everyone; Dragons value cooperation among individuals and work units for equality and social harmony. Cowboys like the rules of the game to be carefully defined ahead of time and enforced impersonally by referees, and Western legal systems fulfill such requirements. Dragons remain suspicious of impersonal law and prefer the workings of customary personal relationships: Rulers who decide what the laws are come and go; relationships remain forever. These three categories are examined more closely in the succeeding chapters.

COWBOY CAPITALISM

- *Sexual metaphors* prevail for predatory conduct.
- *Performance* matters more than personal character in raising capital.
- *Risk calculations* determine access to capital.
- *Competition* is personal and direct.
- *Business actions* are always linear in direction.
- *Markets* are impersonally analyzed, and *"consumers"* are often reached indirectly.

DRAGON SOCIALISM

- *Family* metaphors prevail in favor-seeking conduct.
- *Who you know* really does matter far more than what you know.
- *Social calculus* determines who gets the money from the "kitty."
- *Competition* is indirect and depersonalized.

- *Business actions* are circular.
- *Markets* never get "analyzed" in the Western sense, and business-people always sell directly to their *"customers."*

RECOMMENDATIONS

1. *Avoid all sexual metaphors!* The Chinese simply don't speak about sex in public or use sexual innuendos. Any Cowboy attempts at sexual humor will greatly offend Dragons.
2. *Avoid American marketing language* unless your Chinese counterparts introduce it. Especially avoid speaking about consumers and demanding detailed marketing research on consumers. The Chinese will almost certainly not have such information. It is very acceptable, however, to inquire politely about "how many customers we may expect to gain."
3. *Accept the reality* that the Chinese nearly always approach potential "customers" indirectly by first building relationships with them.
4. *Expect a "kitty" mentality.* The Chinese have very different attitudes about raising money, attitudes that you need to work with rather than against.
5. *Take a careful look* at the following case, TranSwitch. It reveals a lot about how Eastern and Western business models can be successfully combined.

TRANSWITCH

"IC" STRATEGY AND CULTURE IN THE MAKING

Harold Geneen built ITT into the world's largest corporate conglomerate by the mid-1980s. After Geneen's retirement, his successor executed a basic change in corporate strategy, breaking up the international conglomerate, concentrating on a few core businesses, and placing its original line of business—telecom products—on the block.

The impending sell-off worried Dr. Stu Flaschen, Chief Technical Officer (CTO) of ITT and head of its Advanced Technology Center—ITT's equivalent of Bell Labs. He feared possible major job losses among his skilled R&D scientists and engineers.

"Charles, I am really concerned about these scientists. I want you to conduct an entrepreneurship seminar that will be attended by some carefully selected people. But you cannot let on that anybody's job is shaky." We agreed that I would run a seminar on how to improve the market prospects for advanced R&D projects—in effect, entrepreneurship financed from within. The savvy participants would figure out the seminar's hidden purpose.

In the summer of 1984, we met for several weekends at The International Golf Club in Bolton, Massachusetts. After two sessions, Dr. Santanu Das, an engineering project manager, approached me. "Charles, I am interested," he said in his Indian accent. This is his story.

Dr. Das reached America flat broke in 1969. He began Washington University in St. Louis, Missouri, with literally $20 American in his pocket. He subsequently struggled financially through graduate school, married, and went to work for ITT. When I met him, he had climbed out of the straight engineering ranks and up several rungs on the management ladder. When the formal spin-off to Alcatel occurred one year later in 1986, I heard from Santanu again: "Charles, I am now ready."

I explained to him that you cannot just start being an entrepreneur. You first have to develop two basic ingredients: (1) a management team and (2) some exposure to the world of entrepreneurship. Dr. Das needed to work for a small company for a year or two, preferably a start-up. Through our combined *guanxi* network, he landed a job in a Washington, D.C., start-up named Spectrum Digital Corporation as its engineering vice president and later got promoted to president before a bigger company acquired it. Santanu commuted there from Connecticut for two years, flying home every other weekend to spend time with his family. Over that period, we had a number of meetings and jointly studied five or six telecom venture ideas. We eventually chose the high-margin area of IC (integrated circuit) design and manufacturing for the telecom industry.

At that time, chip and telecom technical people didn't know one another or share skills; but Santanu Das possessed a rare combination of knowledge bases. We would have to build both management and investment capital teams to use his skills. My own venture capital firm, along with Stu Flaschen, provided the seed money. We would raise additional money as required through my venture capital network. The management team problem would prove more challenging. We had to begin with the reality that Santanu was an "IC"—just as I am for that matter. Because of an abundance of Asian engineering talent, we would recruit our technical talent from this pool.

Forming an "IC" company within a Caucasian culture presented a number of challenges. Assets revolved around the reputation "IC" engineers had already earned here: very high talent and skill levels and a strong work ethic cultural background. Liabilities involved business credibility and the dangers of failure in mar-

"IC" is engineering jargon for "Indian-Chinese," because so many people from the East have immigrated to America, earned advanced engineering degrees, and then gone on to populate corporate America's advanced engineering labs as well as the lecture halls of academia.

keting, public relations, and dealings with major corporations. We would have to build a balanced management team containing people from both worlds in a harmonious working relationship, so we recruited Westerners to fill key slots outside of engineering.

The Components of "IC"—American Culture:

1. Build on Eastern values of honesty and sincerity.
2. Engage the brain and develop an open model for corporate growth and development, a model that includes informal strategic relations and partnerships.
3. Seek to underpromise and overperform, utilizing the renowned Asian hard work ethic.
4. Cope with the language difficulties always present when East and West work together.
5. Build in East-West balance at every level, right up to the board.

We incorporated TranSwitch in late 1988, a year and a half after first developing our business concept, with the seed money in by late December. In all, we raised $21 million in venture money for TranSwitch before its 1995 initial public offering (IPO).

From the beginning, we recognized the importance of team building. Santanu and I devised a weekend executive seminar series to address business development challenges, such as sales/marketing, technology development, corporate culture, and communications. The seminars also encouraged the growth of comradeship. We ran them every other month for over two years. At the end of each one, we invited our spouses to join us for dinner to further build networking and a support system—called *guanxi, mainzi,* and *danwei* in the East (see Part Four). The end result? The majority of the original management team still works for TranSwitch.

Our early difficulties involved selling our technology, which was so advanced that major potential customers remained quite skeptical. Also, we encountered some internal production problems that gave us big headaches and necessitated

FIGURE 9.1   Eastern and Western Business Practices

East	West
1. Success is based on long-term, external relationships started early and nourished carefully.	1. Success is based on our own internal efforts unrelated to other firms and based on the hard sell.
2. Sharing experiences makes all parties better off.	2. Use the money you generate to make more money and build up proprietary skills.
3. In business dealings, move from: informal relationships to partnerships to contractual relations.	3. In business dealings, be independent and always deal with other firms on a contractual basis.
4. Define success in terms of successful, long-term contractual relations.	4. Define success in terms of how much profit you make.

our raising more money. When these difficulties arose, we decided on a solution that owed more to Eastern business practices than to those from the West. For the differences between the two, see Figure 9.1.

We dealt successfully with our initial production problems by developing a strategic relationship with giant Texas Instruments (TI). A TI division was only too happy to build our early integrated circuits in return for knowledge sharing and volume future business. Together, we built superior chip designs, but we also built a far more valuable intangible asset: *trust*. Next, we dealt with customer resistance by working hard to develop a strategic relationship with Siemens-Taiwan, a large division of an even larger German corporation.

The German parent probably would not have teamed up with us, but the Taiwan division understood how to use informal strategic relationships. Its executives agreed to begin using our chips in its products, once we got to thoroughly know one another. Not only did we benefit from an early revenue stream that made us profitable far earlier than would normally have been the case, but we also became a part of the linked relations among many Asian firms. That led to more strategic partnerships, revenue dollars, and eventually long-term contractual arrangements. From our Asian success, we were then able to build similar relationships with trans-Atlantic firms, developing a global presence almost from day one. Soon, we had design centers set up in Taiwan; India; Lausanne, Switzerland; and Leuven, Belgium. We later expanded into Toulouse, France; Boston; Raleigh, North Carolina; and Milpitas, California.

In the United States, ICs are super-technical engineers; in Asia, we are fellow Asians.

We also developed another strategic relationship on Taiwan that has proved wildly beneficial: an alliance with Taiwan Semiconductor Manufacturing Company (TSMC), founded in 1984 by a Chinese-American businessman, Dr. Morris Chang. TSMC was the world's first pure chip foundry and set the record time for reaching $1 billion in annual revenues—less than seven years.

In our first meeting, we said, "We're new; you're relatively new. Let's work together." Dr. Chang agreed. His company provided us with a critical chip foundry capability that would otherwise have cost us another $20 million minimum up front. We gave Dr. Chang a window into the fast-growing telecommunications segment.

In developing all of these strategic alliances, Santanu displayed a rare marketing brilliance. Even though his training was in engineering, he turned out to be a great presenter with the uncommon ability to simplify very complex technical issues, putting them in everyday layman's terms. Santanu also proved invaluable in leading our Western-style public relations effort. We were one of the few start-ups of that era to hire a professional public relations consultant early on.

Elements of a Cowboy-Dragon Strategy:

1. Marry East and West: combine the two business cultures.
2. Use best business practices: Eastern long-term relationships and Western corporate image building and public relations.
3. Develop sales and supply distribution channels through strategic alliances.
4. Formalize alliances into long-term Western-style contracts once the informal relationships have built up high levels of cooperation and trust.

Today, TSMC has become the largest chip foundry in the world, making over $1.9 billion in profits on $5.3 billion in sales for the year 2000. TranSwitch has done very well also. We are a smaller dollar-volume, higher value-added business. Our annual sales revenues reached a peak of $156 million in 2000, and our market valuation exceeded a staggering $7 billion. And we still enjoy a great relationship with TSMC!

The TranSwitch IPO took place in June 1995. *All* TranSwitch employees had already received substantial stock options by that time; and everybody who was an employee at that time eventually became a millionaire!

> I firmly believe that you should measure your success as an executive by how many millionaires you help create.

THINKING ABOUT TRANSWITCH

1. Could we have developed TranSwitch as quickly using only the Eastern or only the Western basic business model?
2. Why do Cowboys have difficulty making strategic alliances work?
3. What are the limits to the Eastern model for business development?
4. If the combined Cowboy-Dragon model is so good, why don't more companies use it?

CHAPTER TEN

Profit versus Greed

It's a glorious thing to grow rich!
— DENG XIAO PING

Capital is dead labor.
— KARL MARX

Nothing seems simpler than the profit concept to the Western mind. Cowboys don't expect objections to large profits when dealing with their Dragon counterparts. Very different ways of regarding "profit," however, often destroy Cowboy-Dragon business deals. One person's "fair and honest profit" becomes another's "greed."

A GREAT PROFIT SCENARIO

In a meeting in China, a Cowboy executive proudly proclaims that his firm will deliver, let us say, a 20 percent profit within three years of the initial investment. His Dragon counterparts look alarmed and wary and raise their eyebrows ominously. Concerned that the business deal has just taken a turn for the worse, the Cowboy quickly responds that his profit estimate is really quite conservative—they will no doubt make something more like 25 percent! The Dragons now look even less pleased. The rosier the glasses through which the Cowboy pictures the future, the more worried the Dragons appear. The deal falls apart over its huge profits, leaving the Cowboys discouraged and baffled.

> Cowboys see limitless profits; Dragons see unbounded greed.

Both sides have totally overlooked the obvious: "Profit" doesn't mean the same thing to the two parties. When Cowboys learn how Dragons regard profit, they can then recognize that they have not offered too little profit but rather too much! Then, the Chinese won't regard the Americans as greedy capitalists looking to exploit China's relative backwardness. Cowboys won't seem like the next foreigners ready to rape the land.

ALWAYS MORE FISH IN THE SEA

Cowboys learn early in life that businesses make something called *profits* and that they are a good thing . . . within reason. Western teachers try to instill in their students a sense that *excess* profits are earned by *greedy* corporations. But when Cowboys enter the world of Western business, they become steeped in the culture of profits; greed is rarely considered. So they seldom think what profit means; profit is the everyday goal of life. Examined carefully, almost all Cowboys consider just three things about profits:

1. Profit is practically limitless in potential but must continually get earned.
2. Profit is the bottom line for the present time.
3. Profits derive from investments of effort over time, capital, and technology/creativity.

These three things may seem painfully obvious, but when compared a little later with the three things profit means for Dragons, some useful distinctions appear. Dragons don't see Western profits through benign lenses.

Perhaps the fishing industry provides the best single image of the Cowboy sense for profit. Great profits have in the past been made from fishing, but it is an inherently risky, time-bound pursuit. The China Trade also used to be very profitable. Throughout New England, where I lived for years, each seaport possesses its magnificent 19th century ship captain's mansions standing in mute testimony to their builders' business acumen, often in the whaling industry—or in the China Trade. The Great American novel *Moby Dick* tells the story of one fishing vessel captain's quest for profit and conquest over material and spiritual raw elements. The Chinese have no equivalent to *Moby Dick,* and to them the West coerced the "China Trade."

To understand better the meaningfulness of the fishing industry image, it helps to remember the old proverb: "There are always more fish in the sea." Fish in the sea, like potential profits, used to appear limitless to the individual fishing boat captain. With equal measures of luck, courage, and hard work, we may fill the boat. If we lose some fish off the hooks, there will always be others to snare: Consumers are like fish in Western business; both consumers and profits, like fresh fish, don't keep. They get caught in the present and go bad very quickly. While profits seem potentially limitless, they must always and continually be re-earned.

> In Western business, consumers are like fish in the sea: There are always more of them.

The Profit and Loss Statement (P&L) offsets the heady optimism of limitless profit potential. We may fill the boat and still realize a loss if the price falls too low, or if we have expended too much on fuel, bait, and *time.* Or perhaps something breaks down, and the fish rot in the hold. The difference between wild profit and disastrous loss pivots over the abyss of time like a giant, metaphysical teeter-totter.

Every Cowboy businessperson quickly learns that a P&L has three major parts: the top line, the middle lines, and the bottom line. The *top line* gives Cowboys boundless enthusiasm, for seemingly limitless profit potential dwells in its uncertain outcomes. The Cowboy executive making a sales pitch to his Dragon counterparts revels in the risk and opportunity found in international business deals. After all, he began life on the top line when he played "Show and Tell" in kindergarten.

Reality sets in on the *middle lines.* Here the sometimes painfully exquisite balance between risk and reward gets played out in everyday business decisions. Do we risk the capital, and perhaps the whole boat and her crew, for one more voyage late in the season for a swordfisherman, when the weather off the Grand Banks can turn very dirty? Or do we stay home? When a deal with a Chinese company looks ready to unravel, do we pack our bags and catch the next flight to Beijing, or do we write the whole thing off?

Only when all the heady optimism of the top line gets played out against the calculated realities of the middle lines do we have a bottom line at all. No one reaches a predetermined bottom line by stating it as a goal. Bottom lines have to get earned—every quarter. Only the present matters; Cowboys cannot point back to yesterday's results.

Every Cowboy businessperson also knows that without investment there won't be a bottom line for long. Investment means the commitment of profits from the storehouses of the past: capital and know-how. Without a return on investment, there won't be a positive bottom line either. With the advent of Scientific Management, Henry Ford and Frederick Winslow Taylor divided time more and more finely. Profit became shorter term, and investment time lines shrank. *Rate of return over time* constitutes a radical Western business innovation, replacing the old return-per-venture concept that still defines such industries as commercial fishing.

> Factory clock time led Western businesspeople to the idea that capital, as well as labor, should earn a return per period of time.

When Cowboys regard return on investment, they have an intuitive idea of what the return should look like over time. At any present business moment, an investment made in the past has been earning increasing returns into the present and will experience falloff of returns at some future date. The whole emphasis focuses on the present, when Cowboys want to maximize returns; the past and the future have relatively less importance than turning a handsome profit right now. Cowboys invest in order to always keep present returns high, if at all possible. (See Figure 10.1.)

THE WELL MAY GO DRY

A good deed brings a good return.
—AN OLD CHINESE PROVERB

No good deed goes unpunished.
—A TONGUE-IN-CHEEK COWBOY SAYING

A well makes a good image describing Eastern attitudes toward profit. For more than a millennium, the Chinese have been digging and drilling wells into the ground, some amazingly deep down—thousands of feet. The deep wells brought natural gas out of the ground. A great deal of

FIGURE 10.1   A Western Look at Investment Returns over Time

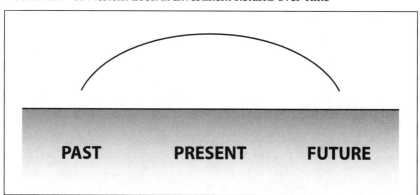

PAST   PRESENT   FUTURE

human ingenuity and raw physical effort went into them. The Chinese learned through experience that a good well could go on yielding its output for a very long time, provided it did not get overused. Dragons see Cowboys as rash people willing to drain the gas tank in a rush to get somewhere.

Dragons learn very early in life that social as well as physical wells exist and that personal survival depends on utilizing those wells wisely, replacing their contents along with drawing contents out. Profit is one such social well.

Profit means three fundamental things to Dragons, as it does to Cowboys, but those things differ considerably. To Dragons:

1. Profit is a process of give and take.
2. Today's profit is largely determined by actions in the past.
3. Investment draws on the past.

Profit represents a small net gain over time from the profit well. Profit always has limits, because it is merely the net gain between taking and giving back within a social grouping—the drawing from the social well and the seeping back into it. Customers are limited in number; they are never like fish in the sea. Only so much may be taken from them without losing them to a competitor.

Social harmony, in return, demands that individual Dragons continually honor and give gifts to customers. Taking too much threatens the individual Dragon with disaster in a highly competitive local setting. Nobody wants to come up with a dry well—even a Texas Cowboy like George Bush.

Many things have been written over the years about amazing ancient Chinese inventions and technological prowess. The best of these works have been authored by Joseph Needham, who has rediscovered much that had been lost in these areas of knowledge.

It follows from the limits that social harmony and reciprocal giving place on profits that any profit earned today derives largely from the past. A current profit comes as the reward for the good deeds a Dragon has performed previously. Try to take too much profit now, and you won't have enough for the future. Never run on empty, as depicted in Figure 10.2.

Investment in such a world comes from the past and draws on it. Investment, like a storage reservoir, naturally runs down; without replenishing, the well will run dry. The traditional Eastern return on investment takes the form of payoffs measured in social harmony: My good deeds come back on me, perhaps manyfold, from my family and neighbors, and perhaps from my Buddha within. I may even grow rich.

POLITICAL ECONOMY

DENG Xiao Ping famously remarked that it is glorious to grow rich. Westerners have taken the remark to mean that Mr. Deng favored some form of Western capitalism, but that interpretation merely represents an instance of seeing what one wishes to. Reality is a rather different-looking beast.

The Chinese people largely accepted Communist rule but never thoroughly adopted Marxian ideology. Mr. Mao and Mr. Deng stand in time merely as new emperors founding succeeding dynasties. Emperors own everything, and they grow very rich. The Emperor has lots of clothes, but he also has fundamental concerns for all his people.

The Chinese have adopted the Marxian capitalist exploitation and slavery of the proletariat argument, without embracing Marx. When capitalism versus socialism comes up, Dragons have a primary concern for equality in the sense of an equal result for everyone *in the same social class;* the Chinese have never practiced slavery but have had servants. Every Dragon in a work group traditionally receives exactly the same salary and bonus—the collective treatment of profits. Equality of result as a political statement contributes to the Dragon tendency to equate profits with greed.

FIGURE 10.2   An Eastern Look at Investment Returns over Time

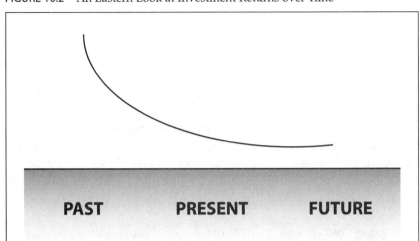

Since Mr. Deng's famous statement, the Chinese have legitimized the concept of a "reformed market economy" while insisting that such an economy creates social gain, not private greed. It is said to foster "redistributive wealth." Dragons have recognized that without economic gain there can be only subsistence-level poverty. Their goal has become one of directing gain from the top to ensure redistributive equality of results, where the Western world creates private profit from below and accepts distributive inequality as a necessary condition for broader social gain. Many Dragons believe that their own system is better.

> The East directs economic gain from above; the West creates private profit from below. The equal opportunity West creates more, but unequal, wealth. The "totalitarian" East creates greater equality of results but less overall gain. Who is fairer and more equality minded?

All these differences come to the bargaining table whenever Cowboy private entrepreneurs and state Dragons meet to discuss joint ventures. Each brings its own historical baggage.

FISHING IN A WELL

No sane fisherman goes fishing in a well, but that is precisely what Cowboys unwittingly do when they bring Western concepts of venture profits to their Dragon counterparts. China remains, after all, a country of personal customer relationships, not a land of impersonal consumers. Even though China has a huge population largely unmarked by Western consumer culture, the Chinese people are not like so many fish to be caught. China may be backward economically, but Chinese society remains among the most developed and complex in the world. Rather than promising huge profits, Cowboys must learn to inquire about Dragon expectations for future social benefits. Dragons, in turn, must learn more about Western investment practices so that precious investment capital does not get wasted.

Although our differences over matters of venture profits appear profound, one Western concept can help Cowboys hurdle the gap in understanding: nonfinancial capital. The Western world understands that several important forms of nonfinancial capital exist: personal, social, and political. It turns out that the Western world's sense for these forms of capital closely resembles the Dragon sensibility for profit and investment, as well as for social harmony. All these concepts stem from the same basic principle, that of give and take. They are well concepts, not sea concepts.

> Cowboys are fish people; Dragons are well people.

Cowboys, for instance, have a finely developed sense for just when to draw down personal capital by asking for a favor. Cowboys don't ask for favors unless they sense that they have already "paid" out some favors to the other party. Otherwise, Cowboys will acknowledge they are "indebted" to the other party—implicitly promising to pay back the debt with interest. The same principle holds for social and political capital . . . and for moral capital. In all cases, the capital well needs to remain at least partly full or else personal, social, or moral bankruptcy will threaten.

Dragons do not distribute favor capital; they give out and receive gifts: Everything in the East runs on gift giving. Westerners have totally misunderstood this practice and have condemned it as immoral bribery. Cowboy government has defined such bribery very precisely—anything over

$100 in value. Cowboys doing business in the East find this a most unfortunate misunderstanding and usually get around it by engaging in wining and dining.

You may also avoid conflicts over gift giving by explaining to your Chinese hosts *why* your company and government limit how much you can give—and then choose your gifts very carefully to please and honor the other party. This resembles very closely the manner in which you can defuse tensions over profits—by explaining *why* it is that your company needs to earn short-term profits in the first place. Then, you and your Chinese counterparts can work together jointly to satisfy both parties, the fish people back home and the well people in China.

> Cowboys swap favors; Dragons trade gifts. It is all very much the same in concept.

FISHING AND DIGGING FOR PROFIT

- *One side's profit is another's greed.* Say the word *profit* to a Dragon, and he may well think of the 19th-century Western rape of China.
- *Private versus social.* Cowboys see profit as private gain; Dragons see profit as social well-being.
- *For Cowboys, making profits is like going fishing.* Markets are like the sea, with many fish in them. There are always more fish to catch: You must continually reinvest profits from the past into present operations. Otherwise, there will be no future.
- *For Dragons, profits come from a deep well.* The profit well was dug in the past and will yield water in the present and future, provided we don't draw too much in any one period. Investment has happened largely in the past, and if we don't abuse past investment, it will continue to yield a good output in the future.
- *Nobody goes fishing in a well.* Each party must explain to the other side just what profit means to its own members.

RECOMMENDATIONS

1. *Don't project greed.* Avoid framing joint business goals in terms of Western-style profits. Instead, frame goals in terms of social and economic gain for the Chinese until and unless you are asked about profit potential.

2. *Throw out the Return on Investment Model!* When actually dealing with the Chinese, throw overboard your Western metaphor for the time value of your own efforts and time commitments. Instead, think in terms of engaging in trading nonfinancial capital, of swapping favors and gifts. Then you will be less likely to panic when a deal takes much longer than your Western training teaches you it should.

3. *Explain, explain.* The Chinese are still learning about such concepts as the time value of money in investing. Carefully explain that investment capital in the West doesn't mysteriously appear out of a "kitty." The Chinese will appreciate the Western sense that capital is a precious thing from the past not to be wasted but used productively.

CHAPTER ELEVEN

Competition versus Harmony

Imagine a broadcast news reporter interviewing American and Chinese gold medal winners at the 2008 Beijing Summer Olympics. The reporter asks the same question of each winner: "Why do you strive so hard to win a medal at the Olympics?" The Cowboy answers with three major points, as does the Dragon. The Cowboy says, "I'm a strong competitor. I strive to be the best. I want to win gold medals to fulfill and capitalize on my dreams." The Dragon says, "I want to make my parents proud. I want to glorify my community. I am proud to win for my country." Self and country.

When these answers appear as sound bites on television, each side questions the other's sincerity. Dragons feel horror at the Cowboy's apparently childish self-centeredness. After all, Cowboys should be part of an American team dedicated to winning; surely, each competitor must strive for family and country. Cowboys, on the other hand, smell hypocrisy; they think Dragons really want to win for personal reasons and are just putting up a front. After all, the Chinese winner really got in there and competed.

COMPETITION AND HARMONY

Cowboys emphasize competition; Dragons emphasize harmony. Competition and harmony don't exist as polar opposites, like light and dark or positive and negative electrical charges. Rather, they appear as the limits to a continuum—a line that measures whether you are extroverted or introverted. Most of us fall somewhere between the two extremes. So, both of our hypothetical athletes compete vigorously, or they couldn't win gold medals. Both belong to teams of athletes who live and compete in a cooperative way, but it's the relative emphasis Dragons and Cowboys put on competition and cooperation that differs.

Competition and harmony each have important roles in the lives of any group or society. All improvement, or destruction, depends on competitive impulses. Valuable social institutions, such as the family and the work group, rely on cooperative harmony for their everyday existence. Too much competition becomes damaging to the social order, and social harms rise alarmingly. Too much harmony produces economic, social, and cultural stagnation—a dormancy open to exploitation by more competitive groups.

> Competition promotes change; harmony promotes stability. Too much of either can have negative results.

All societies experience a mix of the two, or they couldn't long exist. Pure competition results in what Western philosophers call a "state of nature"—an unnatural condition in which nobody cooperates, and theft of life, liberty, and property becomes rampant. Take away the last little bit of remaining cooperation, and a society as such no longer exists. Pure harmony yields a society unable to adapt or defend itself, one ripe for extermination. Of course, competitive America still has many harmonious elements, and the China shaped by Confucian harmony has fiercely competitive families and governing agencies. Dragons picture all of this as the eternal flow of Yin and Yang.

Chairman Mao Shakes Up the Batting Order

Chairman Mao behaved like the first emperor, forcing change by releasing competitive forces to break down over time the old Confucian social order centered on the family. The major competitive institution created by the new "Emperor" Mao took the form of the nonfamily work unit that rewarded the individual partially for all work done within the group. The Maoist work unit, set against the traditional family regulated by Confucian paired relations that made the wife subservient to the husband, proved to be a true liberating force for Chinese women. When the first competitive results failed to yield sufficient change, Chairman Mao released the Cultural Revolution on the land in 1966, setting generations against each other. The resulting competition became too destructive, doing great damage to the cultural basis of society. The young ran amuck.

> The Chinese Cultural Revolution set the young in competition against the old.

SUPERIORITY AND SUBSERVIENCE

That cultural basis has for thousands of years taken the form of a complex of paired relations. The order of paired relations began with the classic Confucian five: Heaven and earth, emperor (and authorities) and subordinates, father and son (a "natural" relation), husband and wife (a "man-made" relation), and elder and younger sibling. The paired relations went even further, permeating civil society—as, for example, customer and supplier.

In each case, the relational order never changes; the second member of the pair always takes the subservient position to the first. The interactions always work as cause and effect—action and reaction. Each social circumstance requires a precise social response, and the same person will take the subservient position in one relation and the dominant position in another; a son, for example, takes the subservient position to his father and the authority position to his wife. Competition of a vigorous nature still exists within such a social order, but *never between members of a paired relation.* Between pairs, competition would seem vicious and destructive and would get punished. In this sense, competition is always indirect in China, whereas it is direct and straightforward in America.

Only one exception to the superior-subservient paired relation exists: the relation between close friends. Here the relation is one of equality. Close friendships between Cowboys also exist, but they sometimes have a strong competitive aspect unlike Chinese paired friendships. In Cowboy-Dragon business relations, the ultimate goal should be to have both parties become close friends in the Chinese manner.

Cowboys can much better understand all of these paired relations when they get put into the context of one Western school of thought: Transactional Analysis, or TA. TA analyzes (a Western concept) how we actually relate to others one-on-one from the posture of the parent, the adult, or the child. Try reading a little about TA to help you understand Chinese social roles. Remember, however, that the West sees the "games people play" as destructive, whereas the East sees its relational roles as the only game in town.

The creator of Transactional Analysis (TA) is the American psychologist Eric Berne, who wrote the classic TA book, *The Games People Play.*

THE IDEOLOGICAL BASES FOR SOCIAL ORDERS

The West has an ideological basis for competitive social orders, the quintessential example of which occurs in America. It underlies the presumed sources for marketplace competition—such things as price and quality, brand identity and technology, and traditions of excellence. This ideological basis is *freedom of expression.* Marketplaces, after all, exist to allow the expression of wants and desires.

The most active marketplaces for Western freedom of expression are product markets, politics, law, education, and athletics. In each, open competition for direct, personal gain gets encouraged. To people of the East, the West's direct expressions of personal interest seem shocking, nowhere more so than in the arena of political debate. Cowboys enter politics to win, and political debate often becomes rancorous. One side wins and the other side loses, once all the votes get counted. Justice sometimes seems subsumed by the fight between notable legal experts. Even in medical research, a seemingly ultimate humanitarian activity, personal desires to "win" by being the first to discover such things as the AIDS virus color all pursuits. Cowboys compete to unlock the genetic code and seek to patent life itself.

Free markets permit freedom of expression; social harmony saves face.

The East, meanwhile, has its own ideological basis: face. Directly competitive behavior patterns get severely frowned on, because they would embarrass an individual and his family. Direct disagreement breeches the principle of paired relations and so threatens the entire social order. Dragons learn a fundamental social principle early in life: Never disagree in public. The popular American television program *Crossfire* will never have a Chinese version.

Cowboys are never daunted in public; Dragons are never rude in public.

Another fundamental principle of Eastern societies follows from the ban on public disagreement: What is *not* said is frequently more important that what *is* said. Dragons always subdue their real meanings under a cloak of what appears to Cowboys to be excessive civility and secretiveness, so you must know how to listen between the lines. Cowboys naturally have a deaf ear to such conversation.

The Chinese will not give a "hard no." If you persist with an inappropriate question, they will answer a different one.

Politics can never be competitive for Dragons because it is the locus of efforts for social harmony. That doesn't mean no political competition occurs, but it occurs as the secret seeking of elite positions rather than as the currying of public favor in open debate. Similarly, Dragon justice fosters social harmony more than it supports individual rights. Science, education, and even athletics are also cooperative domains.

A Story about Private and Public Interest

One of the most basic East-West disagreements has to do with interests. The West recognizes two forms of interest: private and public. Western governments have concerns about potentially "unfair" private interests; Cowboys worry all the time about "conflicts of interest." Conflicts of interest can only exist openly in societies where individuals compete for private rights: A conflict of interest might give one party the upper hand in a competition with another party. Dragons have no such conflicts: Everything is in the public interest.

About five years ago, an opportunity presented itself for an American firm to form a cellular telephone joint venture with a Shanghai government-controlled investment company. I introduced some American firms to representatives of the Shanghai company. The competition eventually narrowed to just two firms. Our Chinese host at that point said to me, "Charles, we think it would be nice if the American companies would work together on this project." That is very Chinese and very un-American.

When I mentioned this to the American firms, one agreed. The other executive responded, "No way! We always compete with everyone. We go it alone." It turned out that his company was secretly trying to acquire the other company, a power play that failed. In the end, neither American company concluded a venture in Shanghai. Joint partnership and acquisition, sayonara. The outcome left the Dragons shaking their heads in disbelief.

COMPETITION AND HARMONY— KNOWING THE ROPES

- A society needs both competition and cooperation in order to survive. China and America differ in regard to the *relative balance* the two forces receive.
- *Competition promotes change; cooperation promotes stability.* Too much of either becomes destructive.
- *The ideological basis* for competition in the West is freedom of expression.
- *The ideological basis* for cooperation in the East is face. Direct confrontations breech the Confucian principle of paired relations and threaten the entire social order.
- In the West, *private interests* create the basis for direct competition. In the East, there are no private interests, only public interests, which limits competitive inclinations and makes competition work indirectly.

BUSINESS RECOMMENDATIONS

1. *Don't go it alone!* Going it alone explicitly commits you to a competitive approach. No matter what level of business activity you wish to pursue in China, only cooperative approaches offer much hope for success: "we," not "I."
2. *Don't fight Confucius.* Your Chinese counterpart lives in a cultural world totally shaped by paired relations, most of them superior-subordinate. Seek to reach a very close relationship with your counterpart—a friend-friend one. Never try to assume a superior position over a Dragon; as a foreigner, you will trigger a massive negative reaction conditioned by thousands of years of Chinese history.
3. *Read Eric Berne!* American-style Transactional Analysis can help you comprehend the confusing world of a Confucian social order.

CHAPTER TWELVE

Contract versus Custom

Good fences make good neighbors.
— ROBERT FROST

STARE DECISIS

Let the precedent decide. Cowboy justice originates in the English common law tradition, refereed by a trained legal expert called a judge. In civil lawsuits, the judge decides what settled law cases in the past have bearing on the present disagreement. In his or her consideration of precedent, the judge searches for the underlying legal principle that has always existed; Natural Law undergirds this decision. The Law evolves slowly over time, but its basic principles remain unchanged.

The Anglo-American system of justice assumes that everyone innately knows the rules of civil conduct, even if an individual has no formal knowledge of the Law. The Law in this sense pervades the affairs of men and women and lives in each human heart, holding every competent individual responsible for his or her own actions. It follows that each member of society is held *equally* accountable under the Law, as everyone knows the same Law and should know the Law before acting. Justice involves the individual. The judge applies identical law to rich and poor, powerful and weak, alike. No respecter of persons, the Law is impersonal, impartial, and blind. In fact, the symbol for justice is a blind woman holding up weighing scales. The Law is blind.

When faced with a business proposition, Cowboys intuitively ask the question: "Is it legal?" When they cannot be sure, a good bit of the time, they call in a legal expert called a lawyer. Cowboys need lawyers because the concept of law has greatly expanded over the centuries to include not just Natural Law and its derivative case law but also a great deal of statute law. Statute law has become for Cowboys like barbed wire fencing in their behaviors where only the law of the frontier used to hold.

LET THE RULER DECIDE

Laws in China don't come from the Heavens or even from the immutable forces of destiny or a legislature. Laws come directly from the Emperor or his new surrogate, the Chairman of the Chinese Communist Party. The very practical Chinese have never had an interest in such metaphysical pursuits as Natural Law. Laws are what the Emperor says they are.

> In America, the judge says what the Law is; in China, the laws apply as the official says they do.

Since the first Emperor, laws have always existed as something to be written and discarded with the coming and passing of each succeeding dynasty. Unsurprisingly, Chairman Mao rewrote the laws when he gained power in 1949. Even then, the formal laws themselves and how they are applied may differ dramatically. Dragons don't appeal to the Law; they make appeals to the Authority responsible for upholding civil order.

At each level of China's complex society, an appropriate ruling figure acts as judge and interprets the rules for that level only. At the most basic level, the father interprets the law for the family. At the very top, the Emperor interprets the law for all of his children—the entire nation. His power descends from him by his wishes to each lower level of absolute authority. Absolute authority, in turn, is necessary to preserve all of the paired relationships that make Confucian harmony work in practice. Every official is an absolute monarch in China, except to the official above him or her.

Whoever rules on the laws does so first and foremost with regard to social harmony. The same behavior performed by two different people may get treated differently under the same law because the specific conditions necessary for social harmony will always differ from situation to

Law is written into the hearts of all Cowboys; harmony is written into the hearts of all Dragons. Each instinctively knows what he or she may not have formally learned.

situation. All Dragons know what social harmony demands. Such knowledge comes from a wide familiarity with custom rather than from formal books of case or statute law as in the West.

Cowboys ask, "Is it legal?" Dragons ask, "Is it in harmony with country, work unit, and family?"

LAW CONCEPTS

Law is a capital "L" concept in the West and a lowercase "l" concept in China.

When Cowboys and Dragons speak of the law, they hold totally different concepts in their minds. The Western tradition of the Law that derives from the ancient Hebrews, Greeks, and Romans holds the Law to be above all human endeavors, subject only to the one God or to the gods. The Eastern tradition holds laws to be subservient to the Emperor, who is a god, and to his hierarchy of officials, and to the requirements of social harmony.

In America, the Constitution trumps even the President; in China, the Chairman trumps even the laws.

The implications for this basic difference are seen most easily when the two concepts of law appear in table form as in Figure 12.1.

FIGURE 12.1   Concepts of Law, West and East

The West	The East
1. Law comes through evolution rather than by deliberate design.	1. Laws reflect the wishes of the Ruler. Laws get made by design.
2. Lawmakers create changes in laws.	2. The Ruler says what the law is.
3. The same Law applies to everyone.	3. What the laws mean depends upon the social situation.
4. The Law seeks to judge individuals fairly and impartially.	4. Laws seek to maintain social harmony fairly and impartially.
5. Judges determine what the Law means.	5. Civil authorities determine when and how to apply laws.
6. Justice under the Law demands the right of appeal to a higher authority.	6. At each social level, the appropriate civil authority's ruling is absolute.
7. Society gets ruled by Law.	7. Society gets ruled by people.
8. The number one concern of the judge is to treat the individual fairly and impartially. Example: Mediating circumstances surrounding a murder.	8. The Number One concern of the authority is to maintain social harmony. Example: Automatic execution of all murderers, because social harmony demands retributive justice.
9. Legal training determines who may practice and interpret the Law, in order to maintain individual rights.	9. Position in the civil government determines who interprets the law in order to maintain the social order.
10. The Law receives its power through the threat of negative sanctions.	10. The law receives its power from the threat of authorities' involvement.

Perhaps the differences between the two legal systems get summed up best by the fact that until very recently no such profession as the Law existed in China. China's desire to enter the World Trade Organization has been driving the country's adoption of Western legal practices and has in turn created a demand for legal services. As a result, two concepts collide in one country.

Of course, the disparity in Western-style legal capabilities has caused great difficulty for Dragons when negotiating contracts with potential Western business partners. The whole idea of a formal, written contract for future performance that contains negative sanctions seems foreign to the Chinese. Dragons view such things as being akin to a divorce agreement prior to a marriage. Although such things do exist in the West, the importance of relationships within Chinese society makes all agreements containing negative sanctions a very alien matter. Negative sanctions suggest that the parties involved never really intended to live up to an agreement in the first place. That would place social harmony in grave danger.

FUTUREWARD AND SIDEWARD

The past is always with us.
—T. S. ELIOT

Western contracts always look to the future. They involve future actions that participants agree now to perform. Cowboys always look to the farthest horizon and expect their partners to meet them there at a specified time. Dragons always look to all sides to be sure that no one involved in a work unit's previous activities gets left out in the present. For Cowboys, the present remains a minuscule point in time; for Dragons, the present remains a vast space for interrelations that require consultation. Behind the present landscape lies an even larger, but very much present and alive, past. Everything that Dragons normally do derives from a tightly interrelated past-present continuum where all actions stem from long-term relations. No written contracts appear necessary to Dragons, because the future merely extends the past. Where Cowboys use written words, Dragons use spoken words.

Cowboys always look forward; Dragons always search the whole landscape.

The Law that Cowboys follow has the future built into it. Even though the Anglo-American legal tradition looks to the past for precedents, it has become surprisingly adept at directing the future. Law has evolved from its sense of a timeless natural order to something more like the working of the spontaneous order of the marketplace. Both have the flexibility to adapt to changing economic circumstances. The same institution in fact underlies both: *the contract.*

It used to be said that market mechanisms had a great weakness: They couldn't allocate goods into the future. Of course, with futures contracts and financial derivatives, all of this has changed. Similarly, law long ago evolved into an instrument for directing future performance in the present in the form of the legal contract. Cowboys embrace the very laws that put fences around present behaviors because of the way the same laws enable them to achieve mastery over the future.

RIGHTS UNDER CONTRACT; OBLIGATIONS UNDER CUSTOM

Something important underlies all contractual activities, whether in the market or between organizations: *property rights.* Nothing can be traded, in present or future time, without clear ownership of the property involved. Similarly, contracts between firms specify ownership shares in all activities. In the West, property rights have become greatly extended as market activities have increased in scope. Property no longer gets limited to physical assets but also includes intellectual assets. In business, the important new property rights fall into the categories of technology and brand identities. Brand identities have taken on importance as technological advancement has changed the basic economic problem from supply to demand.

> In the West, the economic problem used to be making enough goods; some time around 1900, the economic problem became selling enough. That change indicates a world of difference.

The Chinese find the American obsession with brand identities puzzling, largely because for most of the East making enough goods still remains the problem. As a result, Cowboys seek markets in the East, and Dragons seek technology from the West.

Property rights can take two forms: individual and communal. Gradually over the past thousand years or so, individual property rights have triumphed over communal property rights in the West. The American Cowboy experience symbolizes that change. In the early days of the

American West, grazing land was regarded as one huge common field that anyone could use. Eventually, scarce resources created pressures that resulted in laws granting marketable water rights. Cowboys now find their activities restricted by the critical matter of who owns the water— once a free good.

What about the land of the Dragons in regard to property rights? There the tradition is very different. Where individually owned property has become very common in the West, tradition in China has always held that the Emperor ultimately owns everything. The Emperor gives his people permission in common to use what he owns; in turn, his subjects give him gifts. That means that the inventive products of any of the Emperor's subjects, his "sons," belong to the Emperor.

> Until the 1970s, the Queen owned all of the land in Great Britain; the common people merely had the lease of it.

In the West, technological advances have traditionally been associated with private gain: Scientists and engineers make original contributions to technological know-how for the property right to recognition; they and entrepreneurs together take commercial advantage of these innovations for private gain. Private gain drives technological progress. In China, during the great era of technological achievement, the honor and the gain went largely to the Emperor, who also set the technology agenda. In the West, when an engineer turned entrepreneur succeeds, he gets rich; in traditional China, when one of the Emperor's engineers failed, he lost his head.

As a result of these two different senses of property rights, business dealings between Cowboys and Dragons become far more difficult. On the surface of things, the conflict frequently appears to be one over proprietary technological knowledge and markets. Scratch the surface, however, and the conflicts turn out to go far deeper. Dragons have difficulty with the very idea of a private party owning know-how and desiring to capitalize on it. After all, technology in China can be used freely by anyone. Dragons have even more difficulty understanding that a brand name or symbol cannot be freely used; it is as though someone claims ownership in a part of a language.

Cowboys, on the other hand, are used to having private rights to everything that they bring to the negotiating table. Cowboys can do a deal very quickly because they own the rights to whatever they offer. Dragons, however, hold only common rights. When Dragons enter into negotiations, they must always assure themselves that they are respecting the common property rights held by other organizations and ultimately the state. None of these common rights has been written down in contracts; everything is done by custom. Informing everyone involved in these common rights takes time, which would not matter so much if Cowboy private property rights didn't have a time value. Thus, Dragons take lots of time to be sure that all organizations having a common interest in a business deal are consulted; Cowboys fret and become angry as they sense their intellectual property rights ticking away by the clock.

BIG *L* LAW AND LITTLE *c* CUSTOM

- *A nation of laws.* Cowboys like to boast of a nation of laws. In America, everyone receives the same treatment under the Law.
- *A nation of rulers.* Dragons recognize that China is a nation of authorities—literally rulers who decide who will receive what treatment.
- *Individualism versus social harmony.* Western law regards the individual's rights; Eastern authorities regard society's best interest.
- *Private and public interests* often clash in the West; in the East, traditionally there were no private interests. This, however, is gradually changing.
- *East-West business conflicts are inevitable.* Western companies possess well-defined private property rights that they may trade instantaneously. Eastern organizations hold all property rights in common; and society must agree before rights are traded.

RECOMMENDATIONS

1. *Do not* expect China's legal system to support your venture's property rights in the Western manner. This, however, will be changing as a result of the impact of WTO membership, but such change comes slowly in the East.
2. Your best legal defense in China is the goodwill that your Chinese business partners possess. This means that building long-term trust relations with your Chinese counterparts becomes even more important.
3. *Do* put your trust in *guanxi* relationships, not in a written contract. A written contract gives assurance to your American company, not to the Chinese.

PART FOUR

Dragon Traditions—
Cowboy Corollaries

Cowboys possess everyday familiarity with slang terms such as: "You scratch my back, and I'll scratch yours." "Don't make the boss look bad." "To stay in this outfit, you better know the ropes." Each slang expression captures some essence of everyday human relational behavior, business or personal. "You owe me one."

At the same time, Cowboys profess total confusion about the Chinese concepts *guanxi, mainzi,* and *danwei.* These concepts capture the essence of daily Chinese human relational behavior, personal or organizational. "Always show dutiful respect to our leader."

Guanxi, mainzi, and *danwei* have precise behavioral counterparts in the just-mentioned Western slang expressions. Both peoples engage in similar behaviors to gain positive personal payoffs. Different cultural contexts mean that similar games with different rules get played, with similar skills, for different objectives. Sort of like American football and English rugby or American and Japanese wrestling.

The biggest cultural contributor to Cowboy-Dragon differences is individualistic competition versus group cooperation. Cowboys seek individual rewards, Dragons group rewards. The difference has little to do with altruism. The big insight is to recognize the same interpersonal skills at play: *reciprocity, respect,* and *role relations.* All of social history boils down to just a few archetypal stories, replayed since time immemorial.

CHAPTER THIRTEEN

Guanxi (Relationships)

COWBOYS "SURF" AND DRAGONS GARDEN

I BECOME AN AT&T "STEALTH WEAPON"

The big postwar American technology corporations fascinated a whole generation of young Asians. After I graduated from the University of Minnesota in 1968 with a Ph.D. in Applied Mathematics, I had wanted to work for one of these modern, world-transforming giants but not as just an engineer. Fortunately, my dissertation had commercial application for the damping of jet engine noise. As a graduate student, I had managed a million-dollar grant from Wright Patterson Labs to quiet jet engines. So I received job offers from research labs and universities as well as major corporations. I chose Sperry Univac, which sent me to lead a new department in its data communications division. I set off for a foreign land—Salt Lake City, Utah.

At that time, Sperry ranked a distant number two worldwide in the computer industry, behind IBM. (It later merged with Boroughs to become Unisys.) My area, however, hired 2,000 engineers fresh from the Minuteman Project; we did some pioneering data telecommunications work. Telecommunications would become my life's interest in terms of technology. At Univac, I became in many respects a thoroughly American manager—a real Cowboy.

I soon realized that to pursue an executive career I had to break out of engineering management and learn something about the American art of marketing. I had not played Show and Tell in school! So in 1975 I interviewed for a marketing management position at AT&T. The giant telephone monopoly had not yet been broken up, but its executives had already foreseen the need to learn how to market its products in a competitive environment. They had just hired away from IBM a tough, hard-driving marketing executive named Archie McGill. Under McGill, for the first time in 100 years, staid old Ma Bell would have a real marketing organization as opposed to just a sales force. Anybody can sell a monopoly's products.

Mr. McGill, in turn, wanted to find a way to make AT&T's world famous research arm, Bell Labs, more market oriented. He wanted a guy with strong technical credentials to infiltrate Bell Labs and pull out marketable product concepts—to "desnob" Bell Labs as he put it—so he hired me as his innocuous-looking "stealth weapon."

At the time, I couldn't understand why: I had the technical qualifications, but I was this little Chinese guy who knew nothing about marketing and had only recently become literate in American business practices. "Charles," he said to me shortly after I joined the company, "AT&T is not doing *any* business outside the United States. I'd like to explore business opportunities in Russia and China, and I think you can help me." Arch McGill also had a deep interest in Eastern civilization, philosophy, and culture and wanted someone well versed in the East on his staff. That is how I found myself as an entry-level marketing manager reporting directly to the guy one level down from the head of the AT&T empire! It felt like shooting to the top of a tall skyscraper!

What happened next involved a classic mix-up between two cultures. Arch asked me if I could "explore" a way to make "some contacts" with the top telecommunications officials in the People's Republic of China. We Chinese naturally take everything very seriously, so I didn't realize that "explore" meant "do a little research into." Also, as a Chinese person, I took "contact" to mean use *guanxi*—the Chinese term for relationships or connections. I set out, like a good Cowboy, to impress my Big Boss by making those contacts happen. First, I played *guanxi* the American way and by making a professional contact with an older Chinese scientist who had won a Nobel Prize in physics, Professor YANG Zengning at Stony Brook University. I did some Cowboy-style professional "networking."

Professor Yang wanted to help a young Chinese scientist and to help China, so he used Chinese *guanxi* and contacted the business attaché at the Chinese Liaison Office in Washington with whom he had family ties. (China didn't yet have U.S. diplomatic recognition, so it didn't have a full-fledged embassy here.) The head of the Liaison Office in turn used *guanxi* to reach to the top of the Chinese Ministry of Post and Telecommunications (MPT). By a very indirect route, the hookup was made between the top telecommunications executives East and West. The whole thing resembled plugging cords into a series of old-fashioned manual switchboards—a bit rickety, but it worked.

Breathlessly, I told Arch McGill that we had been invited to China as guests of the government. He promptly panicked, never imagining that I had taken him seriously. He would have to get permission from AT&T's chairman for us to go as company representatives, a time-consuming and uncertain undertaking. "Perhaps we could just go as individuals?" I explained to him that we would greatly insult our Chinese hosts if we were to do that—again, a matter of very different cultures—and would also cause Dr. Yang to lose much *face*. In the end, to save AT&T's *reputation*, Arch got approval, and off we went to the Peoples' Republic. *Face* and *reputation* are the East-West sides of the same coin.

In Beijing, we received red carpet treatment, traveling in multiple Russian-made limousines and staying in the finest hotels of that time. We encountered many difficulties because the Chinese interpreters knew nothing about American business, so I had to interpret for the interpreters! They asked if they could meet with me at night to improve their interpretation skills. So during the day I was the "American friend" of the Chinese and at night a "comrade." Needless to say, both AT&T and I gained all kinds of *face* among the Chinese.

Sadly, after I left AT&T, the company shortly dropped the relationship, an action that greatly insulted the MPT officials. After that, it took AT&T a long time to rebuild a relationship of trust with the MPT. It takes a long time to construct a building but only a moment to burn it down.

American *guanxi* works on a professional basis; Chinese *guanxi* comes from family.

SURF AND TURF: A CULTURAL INVERSION

This simple story tells a lot about business *guanxi* both West and East. First, it tells us that *guanxi* is not just an Eastern "thing"; people of the West also have basic needs for relationships that can make things happen—connections. In both cultures, getting things accomplished often depends on making the right connections. Americans learn the old cliché, "It's not what you know but who you know," for instance, although it is only a half-truth. Eastern and Western *guanxi*, however, have very different natures. Look at it this way: Both cultures have similar basic requirements for achieving successful *guanxi*, but each culture does its own

FIGURE 13.1   The Bases for *Guanxi* West and East

	West	*East*
Major Requirements	Profession	Trust
	Expert knowledge	Affiliation
	Connections	Reciprocity
Minor Requirements	Character	Profession
	Background	Expert knowledge
	Favors	Connections

prioritizing of them. As you can readily see in Figure 13.1, we have here another case of cultural inversion.

What matters most in one culture matters least in the other, even though both cultures have similar overall requirements.

In the West, profession has come to matter more than organization; a Cowboy might be a circuitry engineer first, for example, and an IBM employee second. Cowboys network by professional education and use expert professional knowledge as their major requirement for making networking relationships. They will seek out fellow professionals who appear particularly well connected within their professional fraternity. Background and character matter far less, although college and university affiliations do have some influence. Favors sometimes get earned and returned, but a Cowboy usually "calls in" a favor only when times get tough: "I'm really in a bind, and I need to call in a favor from you." Cowboy favors, also called personal capital, have a shelf life—and a rather short one at that.

In the West, affiliation with a major corporation confers trust to an individual; in the East, corporate affiliations mean very little. As a new Cowboy manager for a China-based operation, you have to re-earn the trust that your predecessor had already won with his Dragon counterparts.

In Eastern *guanxi*, profession and expert knowledge matter far less than trust, affiliation, and reciprocity, which roughly correspond to the Cowboys' character, affiliation, and favors. Dragons normally deal only with trusted individuals, which makes it much harder for Cowboys to "break into" Dragon networks. Among affiliations, family matters most for Dragons, with school affiliation an important second. Dragons sense that personal *guanxi* extends back in history for thousands of years; the key that opens access to this long chain of *guanxi* is one's family name, which explains why Dragons express such delight when they meet other Chinese with the same name. Some Americans share a little bit of this sensibility when they regard the European roots of their last names—but the strings that bind them to their pasts have almost always been cut along with the need to protect the family name. Does the wildly popular new Cowboy interest in genealogy signal a change?

> *Business Lunch Calculus:* Cowboy marketers meeting for lunch take the total bill and divide it equally; Cowboy accountants calculate to the penny how much each individual owes for his or her lunch. One Dragon always pays the whole bill. By an inscrutable calculus, the burden of paying for lunch will be shared equitably over time and many lunches.

Everybody in China continually exchanges gifts with others within both personal and business *guanxi,* maintaining the mystic chords that bind each to the other throughout all time. Reciprocity greases "the works" for Chinese *guanxi* in the present and maintains a social calculus stretching back many years. In James Clavell's novels (see the Bibliography), the family founder of Noble House, Dirk Struan, binds his progeny for all time in 1801 to the code of reciprocity. The favors he received from his closest Chinese friends get called in some 250 years later, and the last head of Noble House feels bound to honor them.

> Reciprocity, or "equally and mutually beneficial" (*pin dung who huey*) exchange, means literally "I give then you give." In a sense, reciprocity works like the Western MBA's present worth calculation for future value.

In a sense, it is surf and turf for *guanxi* in the two cultures. Cowboys can access networks when they want to and pursue their own interests the rest of the time. Western *guanxi* resembles a telecommunications network, something to be dialed into when needed. Cowboys surf their Rolodexes looking for the one person with great contacts who can help put the deal together: Cowboys like spiderweb networks.

Dragons live life on a turf made up of many one-to-one relationships in which past and present become a complex whole like a rabbit's warren. Like a garden, Dragon *guanxi* needs to be tended and nourished. The longer the history in such a world, the more complex the *guanxi,* and Dragons have a very long sense for history. Tell one friend your need, and through a long series of one-to-one relations, you will gain access to the people who will move mountains to help you. Dragons love intricate puzzles. Perhaps Dragon *guanxi* resembles the current cliché for chaos theory: The butterfly flapping its wings in Beijing causes a great storm thousands of miles away.

Cowboys talk about "gaining access" to an already existing network infrastructure. Dragons work continually at growing and maintaining personal relationships. One surfs; the other gardens.

THE MANY FACES OF GUANXI

Loosely translated as "relationship," *guanxi* possesses far more complexity than its pale Western equivalent. *Guanxi* means the relevance of any person, thing, or matter to any other. So *guanxi* binds not only individuals together but also companies and organizations generally. *Guanxi* describes the interactions that occur in the physical universe as well. The very seas and lands possess *guanxi*.

On the person-to-person level, family, alumni, and company/work units all exist and function by *guanxi.* No single, simple model can capture all of its complexity, but two models together move a Westerner closer to its everyday reigning reality. One model pictures *guanxi* as a set of expanding circles, somewhat like a map of the solar system. In the very center, the individual, like the sun, finds himself or herself surrounded by a circle of extended family members, forming an orbit like the earth. Dragons call this space *jiaren guanxi,* the closest human relationship. *Jiaren guanxi* usually gets reserved for extended family, but anyone, Chinese or non-Chinese, can potentially become *jiaren* through close, long-term friendship—an informal sort of adoption almost. It's a little like a Westerner with no Jewish blood still being able to become Jewish.

Outside the family orbit, another planet such as Saturn defines *shuren* space, that area where significant nonfamily relationships occur among fellow villagers, schoolmates, fellow workers, and fellow society members. That is why Dragons traveling abroad become so excited when they meet a fellow Chinese from the same village or university. Cowboys use school and city affiliation as bonding rituals when they first meet. Dragons, however, experience pure rapture in such meetings.

Jiaren and *shuren* relationships both exist because they serve as proxies for trust. All other relationships fall into the outer orbit of *shengren,* which means that Dragons adopt a wait-and-see attitude toward them. A Cowboy cultivating *guanxi* may over time and hard work move from the outer circle to a closer circle; what a Cowboy or a Dragon can never do is "surf" these relationships. Here, East and West don't meet.

The second model regards all *guanxi* as defined by the four human Confucian relations. Cowboys may refer to complex books of etiquette to determine how to act toward other individuals, or they may simply choose to risk being offensive. Dragons never face such confusion: Since even before birth, they have been trained to regard every human interaction as falling into one of the Confucian categories. For instance, behavior toward a superior at work has already been defined for a Dragon by either the emperor-subject pairing or the father-child pairing.

Within each pairing, Confucian philosophy has defined the correct and virtuous attitude and behavior. The entire scheme of things looks like this:

Confucian Pair	*Virtue*
Emperor-Subject	Loyalty (*zhung*)
Husband-Wife	Trust (*xing*)
Parent-Child	Filial piety (*xiao*)
Friend-Friend	Self-sacrifice (*yi*)

The very practical Chinese have no descriptive word for the fifth Confucian pairing, Heaven-Earth. The earthly four form a hierarchy of importance in a descending order where *xiao* and *yi* have the greatest importance. *Xiao,* or filial piety, has an exclusive nature and applies to nothing else. *Xiao* demands strict obedience, or *sun;* Dragons will ask, is he a *xiao sun* son: Is he an obedient son? *Chin yi* makes up the closest form of friendship: "For my friend, I am willing to stick two daggers into my chest."

THE TIMES THEY ARE ACHANGIN'

Let us say that *guanxi* consists of strings of mutual obligations. In that sense, it has existed for thousands of years in both the West and the East. The nature of mutual obligation, East and West, has recently been changing rapidly, however. For instance, economic opportunity combined with

FIGURE 13.2 Archaic Western and Traditional Chinese Systems of Obligations

Archaic Western Obligations	Traditional Chinese Obligations
I-centered individualism	We-centered Confucian harmony
Main virtues (I centered):	Main virtues (We centered):
Honor	Face
Courtesy	Respect
Obligation	Reciprocity
Other characteristics:	Other characteristics:
Loyalty to superiors	Respect for Confucian relations
Language distinctions (formal "you"; intimate "thou")	Language distinctions (familiar and formal forms for "you")
Loose-linked obligations from personal loyalty	Tight-linked obligations from a sense of the "we" in Confucian paired relations
Keeping versus breaking obligation:	Keeping versus breaking obligation:
Good and evil	Right and wrong

population mobility has begun to reduce *guanxi*'s importance among younger Chinese. Marketplace discipline has begun to replace family-based *guanxi* discipline controlling individual behaviors. What force will crack the whip in the future?

Some traces of an archaic system of mutual obligations remain in Western memory if not in present fact. By looking at the systems of obligation East and West, and at how mutual obligation in the West has changed, something may be predicted about how *guanxi* will work in the future— for both cultures. Will we evolve toward greater similarity or explode outward, away from each other?

A comparison of the archaic Western system and the traditional Chinese system of mutual obligation in Figure 13.2 highlights both similarities and differences. At least three basic conclusions may be reached here, aside from the metaphysical one in which the Western sense for an active "evil" doesn't exist in the East. First, for many years, Western *guanxi* has been I centered and Eastern *guanxi* has been We centered. Honor, courtesy, and obligation work as individuals' virtues; each Western individual used to possess ownership in his or her own stock of these virtues. Face, respect, and reciprocity all have a fundamentally mutual nature as they work in China; each of these Eastern virtues can only be mutually owned by pairs of individuals. Second, in each culture there has been an underlying need for mutuality, for shared obligations that bind individuals together for mutual advantage and discipline them when they violate an obligation. Third, systems of mutual obligation have evolved in the past and may be expected to continue to do so in the future. Change remains the only constant.

How will present forces for change globally affect *guanxi* for Cowboys and Dragons alike? The present patterns of change suggest something of what may well happen in the future. First, marketplace forces will undoubtedly continue to erode traditional *guanxi* among Dragons, especially for the younger generation moving into enterprise areas. Second, professional education will only grow, and continue to have an international flavor. Young Dragons will earn Harvard and MIT degrees in the West; young Cowboys will seek Eastern knowledge by studying there. A new and global *guanxi* will come more and more into existence, defined by educational affiliations that escape national boundaries as well as by Cowboy needs to build *guanxi* with older, more traditional Dragons.

> Economies can work either by market transactions or by reciprocity. Reciprocity is far older in human history. It is not a matter of markets being better. In the future, both reciprocity and markets will order economies in both East and West.

Cowboys like to acquire things; Dragons like to cooperate. Increasingly, business firms East and West will partner with each other to form *guanxi* relationships. Partnering will balance international merger and acquisition activities; and East and West will grow closer. We will eat at the marriage feast of Western and Eastern *guanxi*. *Guanxi* is personal always. Markets are impersonal, forever. The two will balance each other. That is very Chinese.

THE RULES OF DRAGON *GUANXI*

- *Guanxi* means relationship. To the Chinese sensibility, everything is related to everything else by long strings of ties that stretch back thousands of years.
- Human *guanxi* must be continually cultivated like a garden; otherwise, a great loss of *face* will occur.
- *Guanxi* works through mutual *trust;* family, village, and school *affiliations;* and *reciprocity*—mutual gift giving that reinforces the relationship.
- All *guanxi* relationships are patterned after the four Confucian relations for human beings. Except for some friend-friend relationships, all have a superior-subordinate nature.
- *Guanxi,* through reciprocal favors over time, provides each Dragon with a personal security net against real catastrophe.
- *Guanxi* maintains social harmony.

THE RULES OF COWBOY *GUANXI*

- Relationships come and go; a Cowboy always has the choice to discard or maintain them.
- Relationships are defined and measured by *favors,* which have a short shelf life. Use them or lose them.
- Relationships work by memberships in professions, by expert knowledge, and by networking.
- Cowboys surf for relationships the way they surf the Net—sporadically, when needed.
- Relationships assist individual Cowboys in reaching their goals.

GUANXI RECOMMENDATIONS

1. *Eastern lubricating oil. Guanxi* makes everything work in China, in both business and personal affairs. Developing *guanxi* is not some optional extra, the frosting on a dessert; it is absolutely critical to everything from making opening business contacts to protecting joint business assets. Work at it.

2. *Guanxi has no boundaries.* Personal and business contacts can be separated in the West; in the East, the separation of personal and business contacts is largely a false boundary. *Guanxi* is just *guanxi.* Don't try to fence off personal space in *guanxi* matters.

3. *Guanxi is DYI.* DYI is British for "do it yourself." Developing *guanxi* is "do it yourself" work—work you cannot delegate.

4. *Corporate guanxi?* No such thing. Corporations don't possess *guanxi* in China the way they possess legal personhood in the United States. Working for IBM doesn't give you automatic *guanxi* in China, for example, the way it opens doors for you in America. *Guanxi* is like making money the old-fashioned way in America—earning it.

BIG COMPANY-SMALL COMPANY

THE TWO FACES OF *GUANXI*

The story begins at TCA (Telecom Corporation of America) in 1994. As in the Cowboy Trying to be Humble case study, the names have been changed due to the sensitive nature of the business dealings. What I am recounting combines a number of my real world experiences related to China. The story line has been somewhat fictionalized, but the lessons the story conveys are very real and true.

TCA made the judgment that the way into the Chinese market lay through the halls of government. The Cowboys at TCA would execute a classic "top-down" entry strategy. To do so, they hired a Top Gun.

The Top Gun in this Western previously held a senior diplomatic post in the U.S. State Department. The Top Gun and his staff of experienced diplomats worked carefully for months without any public attention to set up a series of close meetings between senior ministers in the Chinese central government and TCA executives. The American Top Gun would host these meetings in Beijing. Everything would follow the precision niceties of international diplomacy. A lot of bowing and handshaking at very formal banquets eventually occurred—all very highly paid for by TCA.

Meanwhile, over at the Cowboy startup company, WSL (World Satellite Links), Asian Operations VP Gary "Coop" Cooper pondered how he might gain entry into China, without expending a whole lot of capital. WSL faced some serious problems with its burn rate on venture money. The top-down strategy could not even be regarded as an option. I suggested a bottom-up strategy.

Although we did not know it at the time, while TCA's Top Gun worked out high-powered diplomatic contacts in Beijing, I lived out of a suitcase in Chinese hotels, setting up low-powered meetings with local Chinese telecom-related businesses. By the fall of the year, I had arranged meetings for Coop and his WSL team with six Chinese firms. I have built up very good *guanxi* in the Chinese telecom industry.

Only at one point did I cross paths with TCA's Top Gun in China. The occasion involved a meeting that I had set up in the American Embassy in Beijing. It seems that the Top Gun was meeting with the present American Ambassador just before my scheduled appointment with him. His meeting ran over and began consuming my precious time. Eventually, I became quite worried, and I asked the Ambassador's personal assistant to hand-carry a message to the Top Gun that read: "Dear Sir, You are using up my time. Sincerely, Dr. Lee." Moments later, the Top Gun emerged, bowed very formally to me, and stated with great solemnity: "Dr. _____ apologizes to Dr. Lee." It was all very Chinese.

Big Company and Small Company strategies use different *guanxi*. The Big Company strategy works from the top down, beginning with contacts at the highest possible levels of Chinese government. TCA needed their Top Gun to work such a strategy. If top-level agreements can be reached, the Western company then relies on its new Chinese friends in high places to make lower-level connections among potential joint venture partners. Because of the costs involved, top-down really gets limited to major corporations. Top-down costs a lot to execute; after all, Top Guns don't come cheaply.

Top-down can work effectively if top-level meetings yield good *guanxi* and if relationships then reach down to Chinese operating organizations. The strategy requires no particular industry knowledge on the part of the top guns, but that can become a weakness when developing industry *guanxi*. Industry knowledge does matter then, and the Americans who possess it won't have built up their own *guanxi* with the Chinese. *Guanxi needs to be built by every person at every level of negotiations;* it isn't a one-time deal.

At WSL, we couldn't execute a top-down strategy, even had if we wanted to—we simply lacked the financial resources. We couldn't afford to risk losing a lot of money. Instead, we executed the Small Company strategy, which works from the bottom up. We began by building good *guanxi* with Chinese operating companies that wanted advanced American technology; our *guanxi* was industry-specific from the very beginning. Through our new *guanxi* with these organizations, we moved up to meet local and then regional government leaders but never to the national level. Small Company top will always be lower than Big Company top; Big Company bottom usually ends up higher than small-company bottom. Each plays in a different range of the *guanxi* scale.

Eventually, we had a broad, powerful *guanxi* network to further our aims. Bottom up works for smaller companies willing to devote the energy and resources to building relationships with the Chinese gradually over time.

What were the outcomes in this case? TCA built some good relationships at the highest levels through its Top Gun and reached some high-level agreements, but the links down to Chinese operating companies were never successfully completed. In the WSL small company case, four or five joint venture deals got closed, but only one succeeded. Why we got this Small Company outcome makes up a short case in this book called "Expatriates: A Reality Lesson."

The Three Morals of the Story:

- Relationships can trump mere corporate size in the East.
- The Big Asymmetry: Big companies can play down-up strategies, but small companies cannot play top-down strategies.
- Whether you are a big company or a small company, *guanxi* in the East is always very personal. In the West, the aura of the Big Firm carries over to all of its individual business units: IBM always speaks in the marketplace. In China, even the employees of IBM need to build their own *guanxi* networks.

CHAPTER FOURTEEN

Mainzi

SAVING OR GAINING FACE

A FAILED FORAY BY THE COWBOYS

Voysys makes voice messaging systems. My venture capital firm, Abacus Ventures, had provided the company's second round financing. The CEO of Voysys believed that the company should find a market in China; therefore, as the Chinese-American member of its board of directors, I became the logical choice to initiate the effort. After conducting some research, I recommended that we open a marketing office in China as the first step, and that the office be headed by a technically proficient Chinese-American manager. The Board and the CEO agreed.

I subsequently located a highly qualified individual for the position and accompanied our CEO and Marketing Vice President to our new China office some months later for an opening celebration. Everything had seemed to fall into place, yet about a year later, the results looked very poor, and our Chinese-American manager had left to take a position with another American company. The Voysys marketing office soon closed. What went wrong?

To succeed in China, Voysys had needed to meet Chinese requests for technical knowledge about its product, and Voysys had needed to prepare to form a partnership with a Chinese company. The postmortem revealed that the Voysys CEO had thought he knew a lot about China and had begun second-guessing our local manager. He "knew" that the Chinese were untrustworthy. In fact, he had really put the local manager on the spot, eventually causing him to lose a lot of *mainzi*, or "face," with his own employees. The American Cowboys had imposed sales personnel on him, but had not given him the necessary technical support staff. The CEO had also insisted on keeping the Chinese venture strictly company-owned. Our manager in China finally felt that he had no choice but to leave. Voysys ended up owning one hundred percent—of nothing.

MAINZI—TWO SIDES TO THE SAME COIN

Mainzi (pronounced MAN-zi) usually gets translated as "face"—a meaning as inadequate as translating *guanxi* as "relationships." In reality, *mainzi* has two sides to the same coin. The first side translates as the combination of the Western concepts of *respect* and *reputation,* except that in the East concern is paid to the *role* rather than the *person.* It is a little like the army, where soldiers are taught to respect the uniform. The other side of the coin is a calculus for face as a social asset: A person may either *gain* or *lose* face in social situations. It turns out that the West has social arrangements that resemble Eastern face, and those arrangements help to understand what otherwise seems very strange: "Look good to the Boss."

DON'T MAKE THE BOSS LOOK BAD

Both East and West have a similar rule for business conduct: Don't make the Boss look bad. (In Voysys China, our CEO had made our local boss look very bad indeed.) Go a little deeper, and you will find that Dragons and Cowboys use a different calculus in applying the same basic rule. Cowboys use a me-centered calculus and Dragons a we-centered one. The Voysys CEO made some simple Cowboy calculations for his company's gains, ignoring the potential losses incurred in a different culture. He played straight poker and lost.

More generally, the me-centered Cowboy manager knows very well that an outright affront to a superior can easily send the manager to the unemployment line: Overt confrontations with superiors create power plays that subordinates almost always lose. So Cowboys carefully calculate the risk-adjusted personal gains or losses arising from direct support versus indirect challenges to superiors. Most Cowboys instinctively dislike authority while simultaneously hungering after the boss's job!

If the superior appears to be performing well, the subordinate may decide that the better pathway to advancement lies in the external job market. The internal behavior strategy then becomes look good to the boss and the external strategy look good on the résumé. But if the superior seems vulnerable, the subordinate may calculate that the odds favor an effort to topple the boss; in that case, the behavioral strategy becomes look great to the boss's superiors. In any case, Cowboys often give primary loyalty to personal advancement, wearing "me first" as a proud brand.

> For Cowboys, the rule is don't make the boss look bad. For Dragons, the rule is show respect for the figurehead who stands for the whole Confucian world order. A world of difference!

For Dragons, such a calculus would be unthinkable. Don't make the boss look bad in China is really showing dutiful respect to the boss. The Dragon shows a fine regard for harmony within the collective work unit, but that doesn't mean individual Dragons aren't ambitious. The accepted norms for individual advancement simply differ and are much more circumscribed about by cultural limitations: Personal advancement becomes much tougher in a we-centered world. The calculus becomes more subtle, inscrutable nearly, and must involve the patient use of both *mainzi* and *guanxi*.

> In China, *mainzi* is the universal calculus and *guanxi* works as the universal solvent.

If the Cowboy commonly uses the utilitarian calculus of personal gain (or loss), the Dragon uses the *mainzi* calculus of social face. Face-saving behaviors become all-important, for they assure individual Dragons their place in the collective. Losing face threatens one's very place in the collective hierarchy and also diminishes one's stock of social credibility and threatens *guanxi*. Dragon social calculus always contains more complexities than Cowboy individual calculus: Dragons gain face personally by saving face both for themselves and for others; Cowboys save and lose face for themselves. In either culture, face encourages cooperative behaviors. "You scratch my back, and I'll scratch yours."

> Eastern face is a little like Western political capital. Both are dynamic: Use it or lose it.

CHINESE HYPOCRISY? AMERICAN ILL-BREEDING?

Cowboys can become supercritical, tending to search out the (sometimes) hidden flaws in superiors. Detesting pomposity, they may have huge egos themselves, but they like to deflate the egos of those they work for. Cowboys pursue the hidden flaw in others, much as their ancestors searched for water in the desert.

Dragons show what seems to be exaggerated respect for superiors. The boss may be a doddery old man, but his subordinates will tell him, "Chairman Lee, how healthy and vigorous you look today!" They will never challenge him in a meeting even if he says something clearly wrong; that would cause the boss to lose face. They show respect even if in an important meeting he falls asleep!

Westerners tend to see Eastern face as hypocritical. Cowboys need to understand that face is respect for a person's social role, not necessarily liking or approval of the person filling the role. Roles preserve social harmony.

Thus, when Cowboys encounter Eastern *mainzi,* they often react angrily: "How can they be so hypocritical? That guy in charge isn't so great. In fact, he doesn't know anything. How can you trust such liars and hypocrites?" Dragons, in turn, feel appalled when they observe American subordinates openly challenging their superiors in a meeting: "How can they show such great disrespect? They aren't well-bred! We cannot trust them!"

In part, Cowboys and Dragons talk past one another because Westerners and Easterners have come to place primary value on different things. Cowboys rank people according to their professional knowledge and capabilities. Dragons rank people by the *role* they occupy within the overall work unit and broader social order. So Cowboys continually ask themselves: "Does this guy have the skills?" Dragons continually think, "Our boss has really good *guanxi!*"

Cowboys respect a person's expert knowledge. Dragons respect a person's role. They must come to respect each other for who they are and how well they make things happen.

Younger Cowboys sometimes possess the freshest and the best skills; they may be the "hotshots" right out of graduate school. Senior Cowboys may have spent years working on business relationships and not practicing their craft. A junior auditor in an American accounting firm may have better auditing skills than the partner he works for. When a senior American manager reveals his ignorance of some detail of expert knowledge, his juniors react scornfully, all of which favors youth in the Wild West. The emperor has no clothes!

Dragons naturally respect older superiors because they have had the time to build stronger *guanxi*. No matter what the boss may say as an individual, his subordinates respect his position and role in the organization. In China, the better your *guanxi*, the more valuable you become to your work unit. So Dragons naturally regard age more highly than youth. Lowly young men have so little *guanxi!* They are practically naked!

The cultural disconnect over *mainzi* goes deeper, however, to the root matter of how East and West regard personhood. Here all the trouble between each side regarding face originates. Play a role, and you're regarded as a fake in the West; play your role, and you become highly regarded in the East. Don't we all have our roles to play?

PERSONAL OR IMPERSONAL

Once more, we face a fundamental cultural inversion. Look at it this way:

In the West:	*In the East:*
The Law is applied impersonally.	Laws are applied personally.
People in authority are individuals.	Authorities are impersonal.

Cowboys with dealings in China can become furious when they believe that Chinese law is being unfairly applied to them; Dragons with dealings in the West become equally angry when they find that the Law doesn't take into account their circumstances. Both have culturally limited perspectives on the law they face and why they face the law in the first place. Under Cowboy Law, abstract principle trumps the situation; under Dragon law, Confucian relationships trump the laws themselves. Of course, in the everyday life of Cowboys affected by Western Law, the impartiality of the Law quickly fades and becomes personalized: "The law," wrote Charles Dickens, "is an ass."

Cowboys personalize the abstract; government becomes "big brother." Dragons convert the personal into social roles; a powerful official becomes "great uncle."

Cowboys show considerable ambivalence about the whole matter of authority. In business, a manager should treat everyone fairly and impartially, while at the same time showing great individual leadership. Dragons totally lack such ambiguous attitudes: Authority figures should always act to promote and maintain social or institutional harmony. Dragon harmony finesses both Western impartiality and individualism. It also often creates contentment with mediocrity and the status quo. The ever-present tension in the West appears in the common Cowboy saying, "Don't take this personally, but . . ." That is Cowboy code for "I'm going to get *very* personal with you."

PERSON, POSITION, SOCIAL ORDER

Cowboys see themselves as individuals within a society designed to maximize personal worth. Dragons see themselves as small parts of the larger social order made up of people placed in roles defined by traditional relationships. Neither social order is good or evil, or right or wrong: They are simply different. Face for Dragons is a place within the entire social order. Face for Cowboys is a moral category tied up in self-esteem or self-worth. The heroes in the recent Chinese movie *Crouching Tiger, Hidden Dragon* preserve the entire social order against attack from outside the Kingdom under Heaven. Cowboy Gary Cooper, as a matter of personal honor, stands alone against the bad guys in *High Noon.*

Cowboy face is ego personal. Dragon face is social relational. Ego doesn't exist in China; and mutual obligation has largely disappeared in the West. Only by knowing each other's history can we learn the other's point of view.

FACING UP TO OUR DIFFERENCES

- Cowboys and Dragons both have a sense for *mainzi,* or face.
- *Dragon mainzi* is social relational and reflects the importance of respecting authority roles to maintain social harmony: *Who* someone is equates to *what* role that person plays in the social order. In Dragon land, no one is unique.
- *Cowboy face* is ego personal and reflects the importance of "self-esteem" to the individual Cowboy. For a Cowboy, *who* someone is equates to that person's unique, personal identity.
- *Missing the point.* Each side can easily detect hypocrisy or ill-breeding in the other, because respect for the other means totally different things for Cowboys and for Dragons. Cowboys respect the unique individual and see Chinese *mainzi* as totally hypocritical. Dragons respect the authority role that a person fills and see Cowboy disrespect for authority figures as displaying both ill-breeding and a dangerous lack of concern for social harmony.
- *Mainzi conflicts* will get resolved only when each side understands who the other is in regard to authority and individuality. It isn't a matter of right and wrong or good and evil.

RESPECTFUL RECOMMENDATIONS

1. *Don't play face games.* Cowboys can easily fall into playing put-down games—sometimes in jest, sometimes for real. After all, every Cowboy wants to be on top. Dragons won't understand the humor in put-downs and will become deeply offended.
2. *Use the army system.* Teach your Dragon counterparts about Cowboy practices even as you do them. Use the good old army system: "First you tell 'em what you're going to teach 'em, then you teach 'em, then you tell 'em what you taught 'em." Explain to your Chinese counterparts why Americans make a presentation the way they do, make the presentation, and explain again why you do what you do.
3. *Respect the uniform.* Always remember that Chinese *mainzi* honors the role, not the person filling it, just as soldiers salute the uniform, not the person filling it.

CHAPTER FIFTEEN

Danwei

IT'S OFF TO WORK WE GO

I found myself deeply into what Cowboys call a "royal conflict of interest." I had been advising an American firm in a bid to provide cellular telephone technology to a Chinese agency. We faced serious competition from both another American company and a major European company. The head of the Chinese group had liked our presentation and took me aside: "Charles, why don't you become my advisor on this matter?" He saw nothing wrong with my advising him at the same time I helped an American company seek a contract with him! In the West, such an arrangement would set off alarm bells. Kept secret, it could have led to jail time.

I agreed, provided that my American clients knew about it and that no money changed hands between Shanghai China Unicom and me. The Cowboys in this deal thought, "Great. We'll have Charles working on the inside for us." They saw only how American I behave with them. The Dragons appeared very happy: "Charles will advise us both on how to reach a harmonious accord." This is what I mean by *bicultural*—not being an impartial third party but being able to become totally someone of either side. When I am with the Dragons, I become *very* Chinese.

In the end, the deal came close to finalization when the American firm lost its international business VP to another outfit. His replacement, sadly, behaved like a walking embodiment of "The Ugly American." He told me that all Asians are "a bunch of thieves, cheats, and robbers," and shortly thereafter pulled the plug on the deal. The deal fell through because of the human element, not the business fundamentals.

Cowboys put barbed wire around each corporate identity with a No Trespassing sign. Dragons see all organizations, or *danwei*, as parts of a harmonious, larger *danwei*. In this particular case, each side yielded a little, and a positive outcome appeared likely until the joker in the human relations deck popped up.

THE STRUCTURE OF DANWEI

Danwei (pronounced DON-why) stands out as another of those Eastern terms that seems to have a hopelessly amorphous meaning to Westerners. On the one hand, it loosely corresponds to the Western concept of corporate structure—very loosely. On the other hand, it simply refers to the work unit that employs some people—any work unit of any size. Not only that, like *guanxi* and *mainzi,* it also has an active meaning; people work at accomplishing all three pretty much together. *Danwei* in this sense resembles Western street smarts—"knowing the ropes" and "playing the system."

A Home Away from Home

When a young Cowboy first leaves home, he goes off to "bring home the bacon," treading on foreign turf to extract a day's pay. After years of work, some company may become like a second home for a Cowboy. Like a hired gun in the Old West, a Cowboy manager or engineer will more likely move from one opportunity to another, always seeking the best deal for numero uno.

Cowboys engage in both personal career competition and corporate competition, playing two games at once. The change in the international vice presidents at Bell Atlantic at the most critical moment in negotiating a major contract shows to what extent a company can look like an extension of a Cowboy's ego.

When a Dragon leaves school and undertakes adult work, he or she immediately wants to find *danwei,* or "belongingness"—*dan* literally meaning "single" and *wei* meaning "place" or "position." Leaving home, a Dragon desires nothing more than a home away from home, a place in a collective work group. By extension, *danwei* signifies the work group itself—of any size, activity, or structure. A Dragon will likely find himself or herself assigned to a particular *danwei* on graduation and may well work there for life. Nobody simply jumps ship for a better berth somewhere else.

In China, Confucian paired relations have taken the place of Western labor market and seniority systems. The senior members of a collective, or *danwei,* assume a role resembling family elders to their progeny. Role relations define work relations. Getting along with superiors and colleagues always matters more than cleverness in seeking personal advancement. Harmony trumps individual striving.

> Cowboys carefully divide their labor and their identity: one they sell willingly, the other never. Dragons give themselves over entirely to the greater collective; buying and selling one's person is tawdry.

MAKING SENSE OF THE TWO WORLDS OF WORK

Once more, East and West seem very different, and they are. Nevertheless, we also share some things that help us understand one another. For instance, even though major corporations dominate Western work life, Cowboys still have a lively institution called the *family firm.* So do the Chinese. Within the family firm, things appear much more similar. Each culture in this case shares the same two critical institutions—family and family business unit: They never get intermixed. In both cultures, the *danwei,* or business, is almost never family to its hired employees, although it is always part of family to its owners. One exception exists: Work hard and faithfully enough for a family firm, and you become "adopted" within it: You may become like a son or daughter to the father role-figure owner. Otherwise, the Western notion of promotion by merit rather than by birth doesn't apply. For a mere worker in such a business, only "adoption" may trump family.

In China, every *danwei* resembles a Western family-run firm in that work relations, and rewards, get defined by family-like roles rather than by specialized activities. In the Western family firm, the father figurehead almost always gets the lion's share of the profits, even when he has ceased to provide the firm's dynamic leadership. Everyone regards this as "fair and equitable." The same principle applies in every Chinese *danwei*— large or small, state owned or private. *Guanxi* reciprocity applies within every *danwei:* "Equitability and mutual benefit" must over time prevail for everyone. However, a little corollary exists to this rule in China, too: relativity. Each member of a *danwei* receives a *relatively* equitable and mutually beneficial share. That means that the senior member gets the lion's share. Everybody in the same *role* gets recompensed equably as well according to seniority. What a difference a word can make.

Increasingly, Cowboys get paid based on technical skills; Dragons get paid based totally on seniority.

CORPORATE STRUCTURE

Danwei roughly corresponds to Western corporate form or structure. Western corporation and Eastern *danwei* each define a functioning entity. The Western corporate form also defines a precise legal entity, which the Chinese *danwei* largely lacks. Perhaps the best distinction sees the Western corporate form as *functional* compared to the Chinese *evolutionary danwei*. The *danwei*, then, develops far more organically. Look at it this way: Western corporate structure resembles a game played with building blocks; the Chinese world of many *danwei* grows like a well-tended garden of many plants.

The Ghost Town: Three different ethnic groups each stumble into a deserted American ghost town. What does each do? The Americans say, "This place is terrible," and tear it down to build something totally new. The Asian Indians choose to live in the town just as it is. The Chinese move into the town and little by little add onto it and adapt it to their needs.

The West distinguishes sharp borders between group entities like fences on the range. Cowboys have private versus public institutions and governmental versus nongovernmental structures. Each institutional type has its own legal form, such as the sole proprietorship, partnership, and corporation in the private sector. In China, none of these distinctions apply so precisely. *Every* work unit is simply *danwei*. Law defines both the exclusive natures of each institution in the West and each institution's relationship to all the rest. In China, every *danwei* grows freely in whatever directions it chooses, so long as it avoids the displeasure of the modern-day emperor rule by the Communist Party. See a need, and fill it.

Where the ruling board of directors appoints the CEO of a Western corporation, the father figurehead of a Chinese *danwei* emerges out of the work unit's ongoing practice of *guanxi* and *mainzi*. Shareholders elect the Western board; work unit members agree on a new leader in the East. The Western CEO consciously designs a pyramidal authority structure; the

Eastern members of a work unit allow the authority structure of the Confucian pairs to develop naturally within it. Once more, one change happens functionally, the other organically—the skyscraper and the garden.

Furthermore, the behavioral principle that works inside every *danwei* also defines relations between all *danwei* whose affairs touch one another. Every *danwei* practices reciprocal *guanxi* with its neighboring work units in a way that maintains *mainzi* among them all. No Chinese *danwei* can make a decision without first allowing inner harmony to come about through discussion that respects *guanxi* and *mainzi*. And no *danwei* will undertake an action without consulting with every other *danwei* affected by the decision. Decision making takes a long time in such a growing-garden atmosphere; once reached, however, the action plan can happen very quickly, guided by a pattern of organic understandings.

A POSTMORTEM

Now the disconnects in our opening telecom story become fully apparent. The Chinese chairman expected the Cowboys to grow a mutual action plan together with him, because that is how *danwei* behave with each other. The Americans expected the Chief Dragon to do an American sort of corporate deal up front. The Cowboys also figured that a change in their leadership shouldn't matter; the deal, after all, would be between corporations, not individuals. The Chinese leader, however, found the change in Cowboy leadership very upsetting, a change that required a whole new round of relationship building. The new top Cowboy didn't want to waste time in such "wheel-spinning" activities. The deal collapsed.

TOOLS OF THE TRADE

Where Cowboys use the art of the formal presentation to reach across the fences between strictly bordered business entities, Dragons use *danwei* itself. *Danwei* means an action as well as a work unit—the action of using *guanxi* to consult, seek help, and ensure mutual agreement from other *danwei*. So a Dragon can speak of using *danwei* a little in the manner of a Cowboy speaking of using combined informal and formal networking. Furthermore, just as a Cowboy will speak of "fair" or "unfair" dealing between companies, a Dragon will speak of "right" or "wrong" *danwei*. In the East, *danwei* works powerfully, either constructively or destructively. Bad *danwei* lets the Tongs thrive—the Chinese Mafia.

The active use of *danwei* puzzles many Cowboys until they realize that the West has a similar behavior called by a number of terms, such as "getting in the back door" and "going around" someone who is blocking your efforts. Dragons use *danwei* to bypass roadblocks. If a top Dragon finds the way to success blocked by what Cowboys call "official bureaucracy," the Dragon will apply *danwei* to relieve the roadblock. Many things in China cannot be done, at least officially. Through *danwei,* all things become possible.

> *Looking a Gift Horse in the Mouth:* My wife, Amy, and I "give back" to our local community. Recently, we found our efforts to benefit a university blocked by an administrator who didn't want to be bothered by helping the school accept our gift. After a great deal of frustration, I used *danwei* and went in the side door to someone else in the university who would accept our gift.

KNOWING THE ROPES

- Chinese *danwei* loosely corresponds to American corporate structure.
- The *structure* of American business looks like a set of building blocks; the *structure* of Chinese business looks like an old-fashioned cottage garden in which many varieties of plants apparently run rampant. Law defines the nature of one; custom defines the nature of the other.
- Cowboys separate business and pleasure. For Dragons, it is all the same—family and *danwei.*
- The closest approximation to a Chinese *danwei* is an American family-run small business. In each, family-defined roles prevail within the business, and the head member gets the lion's share of all gains. Family seniority rather than professional expertise determines who gets what job and how much pay.
- *Danwei* can also mean the equivalent of the old navy expression "knowing the ropes"—knowing how to get things done by working

around bureaucratic obstacles. In this case, *danwei* is a form of behavior rather than a type of structure.

ORGANIZATIONAL RECOMMENDATIONS

1. *Forget about organizational charts.* The organization of Chinese *danwei* doesn't conform to pyramidal diagrams with formal reporting requirements connecting the various elements. Expect to find organizations in China resembling something more like a Cowboy spiderweb networking arrangement. Learn to use *danwei* in this sense to your advantage.
2. *Forget about formal job definitions, too.* Danwei don't consciously organize work by technical specialty. They tend to grow engineering generalists, with everybody doing a little of almost everything. Don't panic in this situation; a little *guanxi* will get you everything you need.
3. *Don't be fooled by the seeming inefficiency!* Danwei as a *behavior* can produce remarkably efficient, networking sorts of results.
4. *Multiple meaning confusion. Danwei,* like *guanxi* and *mainzi,* can mean a number of things. Cowboys often ask, "How can I tell which meaning they mean?" The answer: Look at the *context* in which the word gets used.

PART FIVE

Cowboys and Dragons
as Partners

Negotiating, decision making, executing—these crucial activities all need to get carried out to make any Chinese-American business arrangement succeed. The business arrangement itself may take many forms—from straightforward purchase agreements to highly complex joint ventures. In what follows, a joint venture arrangement has been assumed as the background to each subject—because joint ventures pose the most difficult and complex sets of problems. Living "in bed together" has far more complexity than a casual meeting! The same principles, however, apply to any form of business deal.

Of course, *technical* problems always arise whenever two parties choose to do business together. Those difficulties become magnified when the two parties involved happen to come from different cultural backgrounds—as do Cowboys and Dragons. However, these sorts of problems can always get solved with relative ease. *Interpersonal conflicts* always far outweigh technical problems in terms of the challenges involved. In what follows, the focus will be on resolving interpersonal conflicts in order to successfully complete negotiating, decision making, and executing for joint venture deals. *If you can successfully complete a Chinese-American joint venture, nothing else in life will faze you!*

CHAPTER SIXTEEN

Negotiating
REACHING COMMON UNDERSTANDING

When negotiations become knotted, people pulling on both ends won't help.
—ANONYMOUS

He who tied the knot must untie it.
—POPULAR CHINESE DICTUM

Negotiating aims at reaching a common understanding of what business we will be in . . . in principle.

Picture Cowboys and Dragons sitting across a table from one another negotiating a new joint venture. The Cowboys speak loudly with an air of authority. They look directly into the Dragons' eyes, conveying confidence and that they have nothing to hide. The Dragons speak cautiously, avoid direct eye contact to show respect. A feeling of mutual distrust, of "talking past one another," permeates the conversation.

"Which of the three alternatives do you think we should proceed with?" the American executive asks with a winning smile, employing a well-practiced Cowboy closing technique. The interpreter repeats his words in Chinese. A lively discussion follows on the other side of the table, the Chinese stealing an occasional glance at the Americans. Finally, their leader addresses the interpreter, who conveys their response: "We are pleased with your presentation and respect the effort that your people have dedicated to it." The interpreter pauses and then presents the summary position: "We think this is worthy of further research."

The American top executive beams with delight and casts a quick wink toward his Sales VP. Clearly they have cause to celebrate . . . or do they? In reality, the Americans have just received a "soft no" from the People's Republic of China. Rather than create disharmony, and perhaps cause the American executive to lose face or wind up having to deal with the aggressive American "never-take-no-for-an-answer" response, the Chinese have chosen the soft no. Like China eggs, soft no's never hatch.

> To a Cowboy, "no" means no; for a Dragon, there is a "hard" no and a "soft" no. Social harmony is very important, so Dragons usually use a soft no— something that Cowboys can overeagerly interpret as a "hesitant yes." It can all become very confusing!

After great preparation and analysis, how has the American executive found himself here, politely turned away without even knowing it? What have the Chinese objected to—the American proposal itself or the way the Cowboys delivered it? What could have been done differently to wind up with a "firm yes" instead of a "soft no"?

BEHIND CLOSED DOORS BACK IN AMERICA

Why did the Americans seek the deal? The sheer market size of a nation with a population of more than a billion people staggers the American mind. Americans hope that someday the Chinese market will translate into unparalleled profits for those companies taking the risks today. So the motivation for pursuing a joint venture becomes clear.

How did the American executives go about trying to make it happen? In the most likely scenario, the Americans focused on building the "business case" for the deal, which means conducting a cost-benefit analysis assessing when the enterprise will turn a profit and just how much money the business will require up front and generate in the long run. The greater the profit, and the sooner it arrives, the better.

The Americans usually think they can persuade a customer by giving an airtight presentation clearly conveying the venture's profit potential. So the American staff works up a presentation that marches to the irrefutable conclusion that the joint venture simply must proceed. The document gets reviewed by successive layers of management and finely honed until it achieves its most persuasive form. Often, "China experts"—consultants and legal counsel—provide additional insight into the process, the lawyers ostensibly making sure that everything follows international law.

The Americans remain aware that developing a presentation makes up only half the task. The other half involves actually sitting down with the other side and negotiating terms and conditions. Preparing for this, the firm likely seeks out professional advice. Unfortunately, however, doing business in China still has something of a mystery about it, and not all the counsel that U.S. companies receive proves helpful. Some advice can become counterproductive, such as the following:

- The Chinese will seek agreement on a few apparently harmless general principles up front that they will later use to constrain the outcome.
- They will use any loose ends or ambiguities to reopen negotiations.
- If your chairman goes first, you lose.

All these warnings and dozens more like them create an adversarial mind-set, even before the Americans set foot on an airplane. They also happen to be largely untrue.

Dark-suited lawyers can become the undertakers for a joint venture. They bury the deal in negatives, one spadeful at a time.

Having prepared a powerful and convincing presentation replete with full-color, three-dimensional charts and graphs, and having been advised on the trickery they can expect from their Chinese counterparts, the Cowboys feel ready for anything.

BEHIND CLOSED DOORS IN CHINA

The Chinese desire American technological and management know-how and American investment capital. Their motivation for accepting the Americans' visit comes from their sense of being behind technologically, and wanting to catch up. They also want American management know-how for systems and processes—"American ingenuity"—to improve the standard of living for the Chinese people. They want the tools for acquiring wealth.

In our example, the Americans have suggested the joint venture, and so the Chinese regard the Cowboys as the host, even though the negotiations occur in China. The Chinese will do everything to ensure a pleasant stay for their guests, feeling responsible for their general well-being. The East practices great hospitality.

Because the Americans will host the sessions, the Chinese expect them to present their proposals and their rationale. This doesn't imply, though, that the Chinese have nothing to prepare. Talking points, which include the official People's Republic of China (PRC) position on the joint venture and all of the necessary activities leading up to its establishment will receive careful crafting. In addition, social concerns relating to *guanxi*, *mainzi*, and *danwei* will also need attention. Don't leave anybody out.

Guanxi dominates Dragon behavior now. What other agencies of the PRC have dealt with this American company, and what has the experience been? Do any other ties exist to China? If so, what are they? *Mainzi* strongly suggests that it would be wrong to have the Americans visit and not inform the right people of their arrival. The right people may extend well beyond the *danwei* that will do the actual negotiating. In addition, the Chinese will mind the details, from who will meet the Americans at the airport to where everyone will be seated, to sightseeing and to meals. Everything must be done with regard to proper decorum to maintain *mainzi*. The foundation for negotiating with outside parties reaches down to society's very bedrock.

The Chinese have also received briefings for negotiating with the other side. Although most of the advice they have received undoubtedly has helped them, they may have also been cautioned as follows:

- Don't allow the Americans to talk you into doing things their way.
- Don't take the first, second, or even third offer if you think you can do better.
- Don't commit to anything unless it has been approved by all relevant organizations.

These warnings help foster an adversarial relation. Different countries, same misleading advice.

Something else may have run through the Dragons' minds. The history of "Western Imperialism" rarely gets discussed openly (especially with Westerners), but the memory lingers. Over 100 years ago, China found itself forced to sign treaties with foreign governments under some very unequal terms—fostering an often subconscious resentment of

Western proposals. So suspicion and even anxiety flare up before negotiations begin. The Dragons will be very much on guard.

> Both parties have spent a lot of time working out what *it is they want; neither party has spent any time figuring out* who *the other people really are.*

THE COMMON (FLAWED) NEGOTIATION PROCESS AND ITS OUTCOME

Both sides now meet and learn about each other's interests. The Chinese ask, "What do you want to do; what do you propose?" The Americans present their proposal over and over again in response to questions or concerns raised, until finally the Chinese respond with some form of yes or no decision. The American side typically contains an abundance of lawyers, with a similar number of engineers on the Chinese side.

The process, shown in Figure 16.1, contains nothing inherently wrong but clearly lacks a collaborative spirit. Cowboys make presentations; Dragons raise questions and issues. Then Cowboys make more presentations. The real concerns—the hidden objections—are never addressed, let alone resolved. For instance, in dealing with Cowboys, the Dragons commonly raise these sorts of objections among themselves, some pretty subtle:

- They kept referring to "Chinese consumers." That is outrageous; a consumer merely uses up and never gives back; he wastes resources. If they meant to refer to "Chinese customers," they should have said so.
- They are so arrogant. It's as though they have come here to teach us. They present their ideas to us without any opening for our input; the whole thing is like a scripted play, and we are supposed to be the audience.
- They talk as though they don't have a doubt in their minds; they are so insistent and conceited. But they have never done business here before.
- My superiors are going to ask me, "Is this the very best deal you could have negotiated from them?" How am I supposed to answer that?

These objections have little to do with profitability, funding, or employment. Those issues, however complex, can be worked through because

FIGURE 16.1   Common American-Chinese Negotiating Process

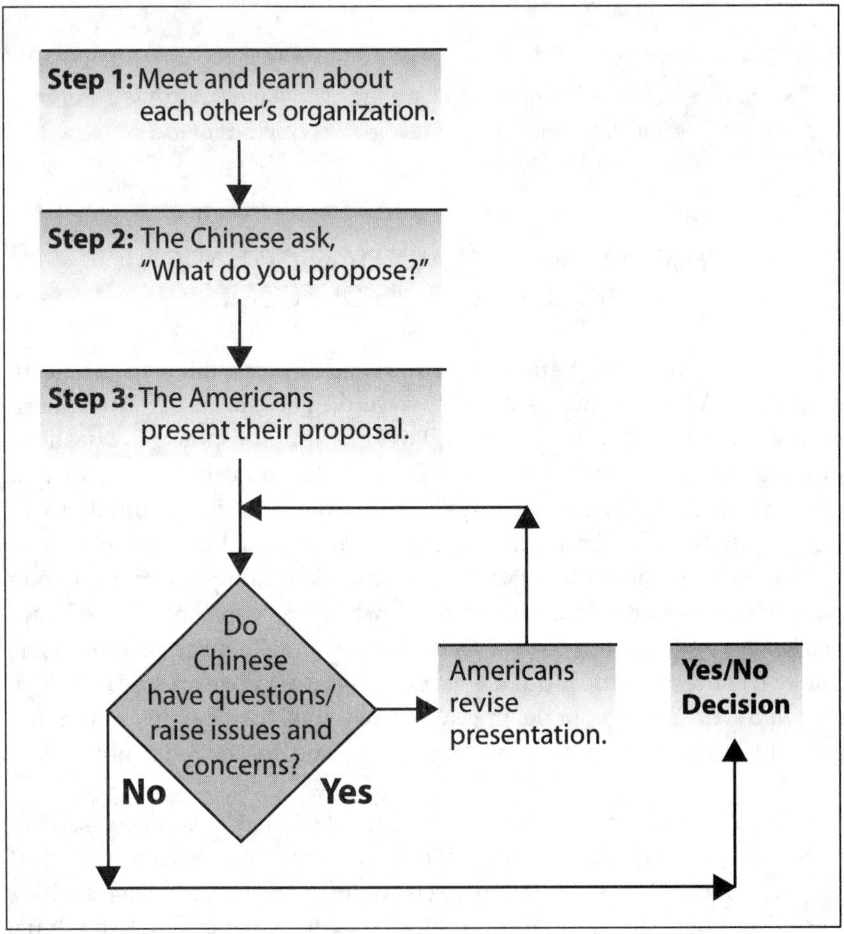

they can be discussed openly. Hidden objections that fester below ground can doom an agreement.

Two frustrations not easily resolvable, even with the best intent, do exist:

1. The negotiation timeline can stretch out very long, perhaps over a year and certainly much longer than American companies like. Given the Chinese desire for social harmony (not to mention their relatively new and gradual emergence into a free market economy), this should come as no surprise. Cowboys need to learn patience.

2. Americans hold back technical information during the negotiation process that the Chinese would like to have. Yet U.S. regulations may prohibit certain types of knowledge transfer. In addition, the Americans may be reluctant to "give away the store" before signing a formal agreement. Cowboys need to explain carefully why they cannot provide full technical information up front.

Even though some points creating frustration and objections may not be possible to overcome completely, most can be mitigated through establishing and building mutual trust. This can happen quite naturally in the right circumstances if Cowboys and Dragons will only adopt a different negotiating model.

THERE MUST BE A BETTER WAY

There *is* a better way, one that promotes more dialogue, builds more trust, and resolves more issues faster. Begin by bringing both parties together to learn the most important or relevant aspects of each other's system. By system, I mean social, political, cultural, and economic arrangements. In addition, as with the more traditional approach, both do need to discuss each other's interests. This first phase doesn't negotiate a single point but instead builds an initial foundation of understanding and trust that will continue being constructed throughout the entire process.

In a sense, we can think of this as "team building," although the two sides will still be negotiating with each other. This sort of team building provides a constructive benefit, although one that appears subtle and impossible to measure: Each side begins to see the other as people—as real as their own family and friends—for the first time. Now both sides can more easily avoid misunderstandings and can openly discuss difficult issues. No exact blueprint exists for this first phase and for good reason: If I spelled out in detail the activities and tasks to get performed and proposed a cookbook approach to them, the most crucial point would get missed: working collaboratively.

Working collaboratively, Cowboys and Dragons must determine *how* they want to learn about each other. Neither side should make a presentation to propose an exact solution, but rather each side should suggest an agenda for a series of meetings *and then review the other's recommendations.* They can then come together to decide what series of meetings and agenda items make the most sense. In this way, doing the first, collabora-

FIGURE 16.2   Sample Agenda for Initial Meeting between Dragons and Cowboys

Overview of Day One Session

Introductions (Part One): Name, title, responsibility; how long you have been with the company.

Introductions (Part Two): Family (parents, siblings, spouse, children); what part of the country were you born and raised in, and what did you like most about that region?

Facilitated Teambuilding Activities: To be announced

Lunch (with many toasts)

Discussion Topic: The three most common outside beliefs about my country or the people in it that are true

Discussion Topic: The three most common outside beliefs about my country or the people in it that are not true

Discussion Topic: What are the benefits to our reaching an agreement?

Discussion Topic: What are the barriers to our reaching an agreement?

Dinner (with many toasts)

When Cowboys and Dragons both start behaving like partners *from the beginning* of negotiations rather than when a contract gets signed, a joint venture assumes mutuality early on—and the water doesn't become un-necessarily poisoned with adversarial posturing.

---

tion-building step itself creates its desired goal. Model where you wish to end up right when you begin.

As a practical matter, a sample agenda for an informational meeting can be helpful and suggests the type of first-session discussion topics you might consider (see Figure 16.2). Both sides may prefer less structure and more free-form discussion, but I should caution you that people who don't know each other tend to be tight-lipped, so some form of discussion guide may help. Formal agendas, moreover, further informal relations.

For example, a CEO might have an opportunity to broach a sensitive subject and turn an "undiscussible" item into a "discussible" one. The CEO might say, "My understanding of the history between East and West tells me that Westerners invaded China and forced China to sign unequal treaties—for example, the Opium War and the treaty that followed. But that was 150 years ago, and things have changed. China is an important world leader today." Or a CEO might say, "We understand that although your country has existed for 5,000 years, in some respects, such as building a market, it is relatively new. We respect your efforts and understand it will all take time." Or a CEO might say, "We have come for the same reasons traders came along the Silk Road 2,000 years ago, to trade in a way that benefits everybody."

> Turning "undiscussible" subjects into "discussible" ones is a fine art form. As you learn it, you will find that the biggest barriers to East-West joint ventures melt away. The biggest barriers are the hidden objections that your counterparts will never address directly.

All of these comments display a degree of understanding and sensitivity. The Chinese will respect such efforts, and their American counterparts will find their reward in a more open and frank discussion than could otherwise occur.

In the second major phase, both sides appoint dedicated people to work together gathering all relevant information for a *joint proposal.* The work may include, but not be limited to, determining:

- Sales statistics
- Distribution channels
- Market size
- Growth trends
- Competition
- Pricing
- Customer studies
- Personnel costs

Rather than having one side gather information, interpret and assess it, and then present it to the other, my approach calls for a cooperative effort from the start. This has a number of advantages. To begin with, the executives from both sides who work together will develop a trust and rapport with each other and begin to understand "how the other side thinks."

When at least two people from opposite sides establish this type of trust, it helps pave the way for everyone else to do the same. This approach also goes a long way toward overcoming the image of "aggressive Americans" bent on forcing their will on other people. It enables an ongoing discussion of important issues rather than having each issue become a major event. Finally, it replaces an adversarial set of circumstances with a real sense of interdependence. Make sure you keep the lawyers away at this phase!

FIGURE 16.3   The Cooperative Negotiating Process

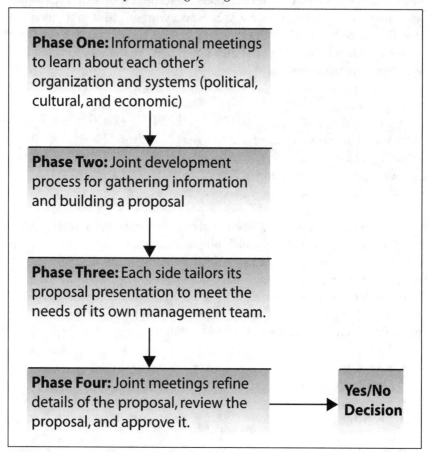

The third phase requires that Cowboys and Dragons prepare a presentation for their respective superiors based on their own internal interests and management requirements. This phase recognizes that information needs, and the way that information gets packaged, must address the unique management needs of both sides. For that reason, I suggest that these two separate presentations get developed—*and that each side receives a copy of the other's materials!*

The fourth and final phase brings the parties together to discuss the cooperatively developed proposal and finalize it with senior management from both sides present. As the old adage goes, "The devil is in the details." In all likelihood, some last-minute posturing will still emerge. Prepare for it. With the broad framework of the proposal having been jointly developed, however, such posturing should prove surmountable. Note that if both sides share complaints from their own organizations during this phase, we know that the cultural bridge has joined the two sides together.

At this point, the two sides have carried out the following joint activities depicted in Figure 16.3. They have invested the up-front time needed to conduct informational meetings that foster trust and understanding. They have jointly gathered the information required to develop a common proposal. They have then worked together to create the framework for that proposal. Now the two sides will much more likely work out the details in the final series of meetings that will make it all happen. *Who* and *why* have now come before *what*, and *how* we can do business in the other country has not yet even been considered!

THE REAL "ART OF THE DEAL" IS A COMMON UNDERSTANDING

- *Negotiation* involves reaching a common understanding of what business we will be in, not just reaching a "deal."
- *Yes and no.* Cowboys take yes and no literally; Dragons give these Cowboy absolutes subtle shades of meaning.
- *Two models* exist for negotiating: adversarial and cooperative. Particularly for cross-cultural negotiations, the cooperative model works far better.
- *The "undertakers."* Lawyers can unwittingly become undertakers who bury cross-cultural business opportunities.
- *Who versus what.* The biggest mistake made in cross-cultural negotiations involves preparing by identifying *what* we want rather than *who* we will be negotiating with.

RECOMMENDATIONS

1. *Do* allow more time when negotiating with Dragons than you normally would if negotiating with an American company. What might take 30 days in America may take 60 to 90 days in China.
2. *Don't* take a "yes" as a yes or a "no" as a no. Always explore further the terms and conditions of a yes. If it's a "no" ask if the work unit

(*danwei*) is saying no, or someone else is. Ask why and what circumstances could turn it into a "yes."

3. *Do* provide as many examples as possible to justify your position. If you suggest the way something should be done, don't make it an American way. Cite company examples from Europe or Asia (so you don't ask the Chinese to make a concession for an American company but rather to simply adopt the internationally recognized approach).

4. *Don't* announce that "the lawyers must approve this proposed agreement before the Chairman sees it"—a statement likely to be the kiss of death.

5. *Do* have an opinion about history East and West, and if you believe something was regrettable (such as the Boxer Rebellion or unequal treaties), say so.

6. *Don't* under any circumstances say "take it or leave it."

7. *Do* use interpreters who are *bicultural* as well as *bilingual*.

8. *Don't* take the interpreter's translation at face value. Ask for clarification, repeatedly if necessary.

9. *Do* brush up on your understanding of American culture and history. Many Dragons express surprise to learn that although America is a relatively new nation, its democratic style of government has its origins in ancient Greece. The Chinese respect history and longevity, so let them know just how far back American roots stretch.

CHAPTER SEVENTEEN

Decision Making
COWBOY WAY, DRAGON WAY, AND VC WAY

> Decision making involves running the business in detail—on paper.

COMING IN LIKE A COWBOY

Taiwan faces a difficult challenge in making its citizens' telephone numbers transportable (see the NeuStar case). I felt very certain that both government and private telecom leaders would eagerly jump at what my client NeuStar could do in this area and that I could close a deal quickly there. After all, I grew up on Taiwan. I had known these people for many years, and I had previously helped start the venture capital industry on the island. On Taiwan, I have great *guanxi*.

So I arranged a meeting with them. I had my presentation all worked out and went through it flawlessly, showing them just why they should do business with NeuStar. When I finished, my guests made some polite remarks about the proposal being very interesting and that they would have to study it further. I realized that I was getting a "soft no"!

Inside of myself, I grew very angry. How could these people, my *friends*, treat me this way? They have known me for years! Then I realized what I had done wrong: I had come into the meeting acting like a Cowboy!

THE FATAL 18 INCHES BETWEEN
THE HEAD AND THE HEART

Only 18 inches separates the human head from the heart, but sometimes that might as well be half the distance around the world. When it

Cowboys think decisions through; Dragons mull them over. That is the little, 18-inch difference that often becomes unbridgeable.

comes to decision making between Cowboys and Dragons, 18 little inches can destroy a potentially fruitful deal, for two fundamental reasons. First, one side favors rational arguments whereas the other side favors highly sensitive intuitions. Second, each side expects the other side to make decisions the way it does and takes offense when the other side doesn't. Very often, both sides fail to follow the old adage about how to catch fish: First, you must think like a fish.

The Uncommon Leadership Skill: Great generals have the uncommon gift of getting into the heart and mind of the opposing general, of knowing what the enemy will do even before he himself does. Look at the American Civil War General Lee (I am not related to him!) or the Chinese author of *The Art of War,* Sun Tzu.

Figure 17.1 compares decision making in the East and West. For each party, the same six basic dimensions to decision making come into play, but the details differ dramatically.

At the very beginning, each side seeks to inform itself about aspects of a potential business deal. Cowboys, however, concentrate on "hard," statistical sorts of data largely related to the nature of the market and its size. Dragons want to know about any *danwei* history of working with the Cowboys, and they want to know their colleagues' technological needs. The very different informational demands of each party requires, in turn, a different sort of analytical process. Cowboys crunch numbers. Dragons intuit the subtlest of nuanced responses from the broadest *danwei* group. Then, Cowboys think, and Dragons ruminate. One process evidences the lightning speed of a computer, the other the deliberate slowness of a cow's digestive organs.

Cowboys don't work to the nanosecond, but they have a pretty precise idea of how long proposal generation and deal making should take. Cowboys are a breed for whom time stands as the enemy. They explode from the starting gate on any project but run out of energy quickly.

Dragons, on the other hand, don't even measure progress in units of time, but on the strength of accumulating harmony. They settle into a

FIGURE 17.1   How Cowboys and Dragons Make Decisions

The West	*The East*
Step 1. Gather information: Objective, statistical data, systematically recorded Assumptions amenable to proof	Step 1. Gather information: Word-of-mouth, empirical findings, chronologically stored in memory Processed by gut feeling
Step 2. Analyze information: A rapid process. "What do you think?" Answer is in the numbers A logical response to data	Step 2. Mull over information: A drawn-out process. "How do you feel?" Answer in group body language A holistic response to the *danwei*
Step 3. Create a relationship between product and market.	Step 3. Relationship between product and market exists (within *guanxi*) to use if we wish to.
Step 4. Give the project a time frame: Short-term/midcourse corrections	Step 4. Give *guanxi* time to work: Indeterminate (but longer) term with careful consideration of the whole plan
Step 5. Hand off to decision maker: Locus of decision is individual. Decision made by top executive.	Step 5. Decision-making: Locus of decision is the *danwei.* Decision made by consensus (hard to know at what level of *danwei).*
Step 6. Channel energy: Early burst of energy to project; fall off if delays occur.	Step 6. Channel energy: Slow buildup of energy over project; enthusiasm grows as relations form.

comfortable pace for the long haul and they build energy as the race progresses to the finish. They are the marathon runners of the business world. Sprinters and long-distance runners always have trouble keeping together.

Cowboys are sprinters; Dragons are long-distance runners.

Cowboys sometimes appear to follow the principle of impetuosity: Do something, even if it's wrong; we can always fix it later. Cowboys want to execute a deal quickly and then make midcourse corrections as needed. Dragons want to work out all of the future details very carefully. The reason is simple: What Cowboys can regard as a simple mistake to get fixed, Dragons will experience as a serious breach of harmony that will occur in *danwei* relationships later on. Dragons need to get it right the first time.

The desire for harmony also explains why the locus of the actual decision appears so diffuse to a Westerner. Because every Dragon must concur in a decision, the final piece in the overall process may come from anywhere. On the other hand, every Cowboy knows who runs the ranch. This is true even in government. The whole world knows when George W. Bush has reached a decision on some matter; nobody, in the West at least, can know for sure where a Chinese government decision emanated from. In the West, the precise decision point in time emanates from the corporation's head. In China, the decision rises up from the belly of the beast.

Does this mean that the Western business process is inherently better—more precise or faster? Not necessarily. The Chinese process, in fact, may sometimes work more smoothly and quickly. For Dragons doing *danwei,* no time needs to be taken to *create* a market; the market already exists once the decision has been reached. Dragons also use *danwei* to eliminate roadblocks, ahead of time. While Cowboys can reach decisions faster, Dragons can sometimes make the whole decision-making *and* execution time period shorter. The Cowboys are hares, the Dragons tortoises. Everybody knows who won the fabled race.

How can a binding courtship be created out of so much potential confusion? The answer is simple: Each party needs to explain up front to the other party *exactly how it makes decisions.* With mutual understanding established, the courtship can proceed to a successful union and lay hybrid eggs that hatch!

A POSTMORTEM

We can now go back to the opening business scenario and better understand what went wrong when I rode into the Taiwan meeting. I made a near-fatal mistake: I assumed that because my counterparts knew me well,

I could short-circuit the Eastern manner of reaching decisions. I had to apologize to my friends for appearing too eager to reach an agreement. Then, I had to go back to the very beginning and re-establish *guanxi.*

> *Ritual Matters:* Make friends at each step along the way. You don't deal with the same people from step to step. The process is always the same:
>
> 1. Know each other.
> 2. Accept each other.
> 3. Become friends.
> 4. Work together.

That done, we all proceeded through the entire cooperative negotiating process that defined what business we would be in together. After that, a joint work group had to actually run the business on paper. All the while, time ticked away, and the Dragons worked out many potential disharmonies among the numerous *danwei* involved. During that whole period, their leadership did a lot of ruminating over the decision. Finally, after a year of work and just before this chapter was written, the Taiwanese began to accept NeuStar's approach to number administration.

VENTURE CAPITALISTS ARE LIKE DRAGONS

I am a long-term member of a Cowboy posse nicknamed the VCs. The Venture Capitalists ride into town looking to rescue infant companies from financial famine. All kidding aside, we aren't "Vulture Capitalists"as some entrepreneurs believe! The way venture capitalists behave can, however, appear very confusing to Cowboy entrepreneurs. The individual entrepreneur believes that the VCs want to see great technology, the entrepreneur puts it on display, like a peacock. The VCs, it turns out, couldn't care less for technology per se; we look at the company's *people.* We want to know: Does the company have a great management team?

> VCs act more like Dragons than like Cowboys.

When confronted by the core question in an industry—which venture do we invest in—a VC will say that the decision process resembles a sequential coin-tossing game. We keep tossing the coin—looking at the choices—and asking ourselves a basic question: Do we *feel* we're there yet? If not, we keep on tossing the coin. It's much more like ruminating than analyzing. Cowboys don't ruminate.

VCs use another tool that Cowboys rarely understand: the five-finger principle. A VC can count on one hand everything we need to see to do a deal: people, people, people, market, and technology—*in that order*. Cowboy entrepreneurs use the same categories, but they reverse the order. When a Cowboy techie performs due diligence on a potential partner or merger candidate, he or she always focuses on technology, technology, and technology, and then markets and people; people have importance only as producers of technology. When we VCs do due diligence, we look primarily at management. And the CEO must want to get rich!

So, Cowboys and VCs can look at the famous Pieter Breughel painting of Icarus falling from the skies and see very different things. Icarus, remember, was the mythic Greek whose father made wings of eagle feathers for them to reach the gods—the first flying machines. Icarus flew too high, and the sun melted the wax holding the feathers in place. Cowboys look at the painting and see a design failure in the wing area; we VCs look and see a test team screwup.

> *Basic Realities:* The West is technology thick; the East is technology thin. The West is used to technical competence; the East is used to people competence.

When it comes to an East-West deal, Cowboys place technological dominance first, market analysis second, and understanding the other side a distant third. Cowboys need to reverse that order when dealing with Dragons or the VCs.

WHO BUYS AND WHO SELLS?

VCs have an old saying: "We all have the same thing—money. So what makes us different? If you take *my* money, you also get *me*. Who do you want—me or some other VC?" Again we resemble Dragons more than

Cowboys. We can invest in any technology: We possess people competency. However, when we do invest, who buys and who sells?

In any transaction, how can you tell the buyer from the seller? The buyer is the one in control; the buyer makes the final decision. In the West, we call it customer sovereignty. In the East, it is the superior position in a Confucian relationship.

The knee-jerk response, of course, is that the VC firm buys—company shares—and the entrepreneurial firm sells. That is very Western. We're in control, most VCs think. We decide who gets the money.

Perhaps because I grew up on mainland China and then Taiwan, I see the transactional reality differently: The entrepreneur is always the buyer; the VC is the seller. I, as a VC, am selling my capital and *me*. The entrepreneur decides whether to buy from me, or from someone else.

The same principle applies to East-West partnerships. Cowboys want to think they are the buyers—buying into China's vast market. In reality, Cowboys are at least as much sellers as buyers, and the Dragons decide *whom* they wish to buy from as much as they decide *what* technology to purchase. The Dragons are the buyers. Confucius would have smiled.

DECISIONS, DECISIONS, DECISIONS

- *Negotiating* reaches a common understanding of what business we will be in. *Decision making* actually runs the business in detail *on paper*.
- *At each step,* the need to make friends arises all over again, because the same people aren't involved in negotiating, decision making, or even executing for that matter.
- Dragons and Cowboys reach decisions in very different ways. To avoid hopeless confusion, each party must *explain to the other how it goes about making decisions.*
- Cowboys reach decisions *with the head.* Everything is rational: "I *think* it is a good decision." Dragons reach decisions *with the heart.* Everything is intuitive: "I *feel* good about the decision."
- *The time frame* matters to Cowboys; *harmony among the danwei* matters to Dragons.

- As a result, Cowboys can *make decisions quickly* but frequently need to make a lot of midcourse corrections during execution. Dragons *think things through.* As a result, although Dragons take longer to decide, execution often goes much faster. Neither way is inherently better; when the two parties work together, the best of both worlds can get realized.

RECOMMENDATIONS

1. *Always consider* guanxi. Cowboys who think in terms of *corporate* relations can easily forget that in China all relations are *personal.* So it is easy to overlook the need to build new *guanxi* at every step of a business venture. As you go from negotiating to decision making to executing, new people become involved. First, you must build *guanxi* with them; then you can proceed on business matters.
2. *Different processors.* Cowboys and Dragons use different internal information-processing principles. To avoid hopeless confusion during decision making, *explain* how you make decisions in the West, and *listen* to how Dragons make decisions in the East.
3. *Priorities matter.* Our priorities drive our deal-making behaviors, but Cowboys and Dragons have different priorities! Cowboys worry about *time,* whereas Dragons worry about *harmony.* Explain your time concerns and listen to the Dragons' harmony matters.
4. *Now run the business on paper.* Only when all of the "getting-to-know-you" matters have been worked out can the nuts and bolts of actual decision making begin. The nuts and bolts of decision making involve running the business *together* on paper.

CHAPTER EIGHTEEN

Executing

FROM WORDS TO DEEDS

Executing a business plan is all about marrying people to money.

NINE MONTHS IN THE SHANGHAI HILTON

Bob Jones of WSL (names have been changed) learned about conflict firsthand. In 1994, at age 26, he joined the WSL-SSTIC joint venture project as a business development analyst (see "A Cowboy Trying to be Humble"). He lived "temporarily" in the Shanghai Hilton—for nine months as it turned out. You can guess what his room looked like.

WSL did six joint ventures in China, but only the one in Shanghai prospered. There, YU Jian Guo, a local Chinese, became CEO. In all the other joint ventures, Americans had overall charge. Under Mr. Yu, WSL guys served as CFO and head of marketing. Bob Jones developed the actual operating plan, working closely with his Chinese counterparts. He had to do a lot of Show and Tell work to get the budget they needed out of the joint venture's deep pockets. He also had a lot of conflicts with his Dragon counterparts over budget line items to get resolved. More of the conflicts came from the Cowboys than from the Dragons. Conflict became his daily companion.

In 1997, after a $25 million investment, WSL pulled the plug on its China effort because of the low likelihood of ever earning a return there. The Chinese-American CFO of the Shanghai venture stayed on, however, after SSTIC bought the entire unit from WSL. It still operates successfully today as SVC. Bob Jones moved on to work at NeuStar.

FIGURE 18.1   Building a Team

How the West Builds a Team	How the East Builds a Team
First, "corporate" picks the leader.	First, the superior picks the whole team.
Second, the leader chooses his underlings.	Second, the team leader emerges from a *mainzi* process.
Third, the leader decides a budget request.	Third, the team decides on a budget request.
The result: Quick outcome Individual accountability High authority High accountability	The result: Slow outcome Group accountability High authority Low accountability

MARRYING PEOPLE TO MONEY

Executing is all about the process of marrying people to money. At WSL, the joint venture projects went well at first because we had deep pockets behind us. It turned out to be something of a "marriage of convenience" that didn't last.

Executing involves three fundamental steps, each performed in different ways by the East and the West. Before the actual marriage can occur, the first execution step must be completed—building a team. To begin, each side puts together a team. Then, from those teams, a joint team gets created. The difficulties start here.

Building a joint team requires that decisions get made with regard to *which side will become responsible for what functions.* Under ordinary, domestic circumstances, this can be tough enough; it gets far tougher when two different cultures are involved. Team building simply doesn't work the same way in the East and the West. (See Figure 18.1.)

Cowboys focus on who will be the *Boss.* Dragons focus on the makeup of the *whole team*—how well will it work together in harmony? Cowboys don't worry overly much about such things: The Top Cowboy carries a Colt .45—a Peacemaker—in the form of hire-and-fire authority.

The strength of Cowboy teams comes from their *high* levels of accountability; conversely, the weakness in Dragon teams comes from their *low* levels of accountability. On the other hand, Cowboy teams may contain

FIGURE 18.2   Acquiring a Budget

How Cowboys Do It	How Dragons Do It

Show and Tell—The Big Tale:
    A dream story
    "This is what I can do."
	The allocation story:
	    The humble request
	    "How much will you give me to
	    do the job?"

Not "How much is there?" but
    "This is how much I need."
	Not "This is how much I need," but
	    "How much is allocated?"

simmering conflicts just below the surface, whereas Dragon teams may achieve high levels of group harmony. Try to find the best of both worlds.

Cowboys instinctively want their guys to fill all the top positions. After all, we're the people with the technology and the capital. Dragons, in turn, see such demands as just another form of Yankee imperialism: Once more, they want to conquer us through superior technology and by capturing our markets. Cowboys want all the *Boss* roles.

Capturing the Boss position can become a hollow victory, because your Dragon counterparts may lose a lot of face. Your venture may lose all the advantages of leadership by someone who knows how to work with government agencies. Favorable *guanxi* may just melt away like overheated sealing wax.

Is there a rule for effective joint venture team building? Yes. Appoint a Dragon as chairman, and let a Cowboy control the purse strings. In the WSL example above, only the Shanghai joint venture had a Chinese CEO; the other ventures had imported Cowboys in the lead. The Shanghai CFO and marketing head were Chinese-Americans. Only the Shanghai venture succeeded (see "Expatriates: A Reality Lesson" for more details). Today, among other activities, it administers the Shanghai lottery system, an activity that requires a lot of trust and competence.

GETTING THE MONEY

Once the joint management team has been created, the second execution step may begin—acquiring the budget. Once more, the same basic step works differently for Cowboys and for Dragons, as shown in Figure 18.2. Dragons regard the problem as being one in which the "grandfather" banker has a piggybank with only so much money in it altogether. Dragons ask, "How much is in the piggybank for our project?" They see the budget as limited—there is only so much to go around for everyone's projects. The allocation game gets played from a we-centered perspective: "We don't want to ask for too much, because that might hurt others." So Dragons ask, "How much will you allocate to us to get the job done?" For Dragons, life is a zero-sum game.

Cowboys never picture a grandfather with a piggybank. They picture a dream—the bigger the better. Cowboys don't live in a zero-sum game world; they live in a world of nearly infinite possibilities: "If I can dream it, someone can finance it." Special purpose Cowboys, such as venture capitalists, exist to fill in the money holes. For Cowboys, the "Big Dream" is limited by only one reality: making a profit on the budget amount. Show me the profit projection, and I'll give you the money.

Understandably, budget acquisition can badly fracture *guanxi* on a joint venture team unless handled carefully. Dragons on the team resist asking for money for such "luxuries" as marketing; Cowboys chafe under the Dragons' silly frugality. Such conflicts can get resolved only one way—by working through the friendship model all over again: Get to know each other. Get to know *why* each side regards the budget the way it does. Accept each other for who each is: Nobody is either right or wrong. Work together to resolve each money issue. Each small resolution will come painfully at first, like walking in tight, new shoes.

THIS IS THE WAY WE DO THINGS

Tactics always reflect management style.

The third and last execution step involves tactics. Business strategy has already gotten set in the negotiating and decision-making steps. Only tactics remain—who does what, when, with which results? Tactical styles characteristic of East and West are displayed in Figure 18.3. Cowboys always assign tactical responsibilities by individual. On a Cowboy team, everybody knows his or her own assignment very well. Nobody wants to know much about other managers' assignments. For Cowboys, good managers respect the fences between responsibility areas, because responsibilities are personal and conflicts over them should be avoided. Don't get into "turf wars."

FIGURE 18.3   Tactical Styles: West and East

The West	The East
Clearly define *individual* assignments and then execute them.	This is what *we* will do.
Each individual is clear about his or her own assignment, and is not clear about other's.	Everybody knows where we're going and does a little bit.
Results: Speed and efficiency Vulnerability to Big Mistakes	Results: Slowness and inefficiency No Big Mistakes

From a very early age, a Cowboy learns to protect his or her own turf, and Dragons learn that there is no private turf.

For Dragons, all responsibilities get held in common: Everybody knows where *we* are going and how we're going to get there. Instead of a single manager shouldering an entire responsibility, everyone does a little bit of everything. Don't break social harmony by trying to go it alone. The tallest sticks in the bundle get pounded down.

Clearly, East and West management styles differ greatly, which means a lot of potential conflict on a joint venture team as tactics get developed. One principle about conflicts certainly applies here: The earlier you deal with them, the simpler they are to resolve. This begs a basic question, however: *How* do I deal with tactical conflict in the first place?

Two rules apply. The first cautions you about a fundamental, erroneous assumption, that your counterparts from the other culture do things the same way you do. Cowboys who operate from a position of great individual autonomy have a much greater vulnerability in this regard. They grow up focused on their own actions and never think to question how others might undertake action. The Marlboro Man never asks anyone how to do the job.

Beware of how the other party is used to doing things.

The second rule locates the responsibility for clarifying how you do things. Human nature assumes that others will see how you do things or ask how you do them. Again, this seems to be truer for I-centered Cowboys than for we-centered Dragons. Waiting to be asked, however, will never work: You must first tell the other party how it is that you do things before anything ever gets done. Tell; don't wait to be asked.

It's *your* responsibility to explain how you do things—not the other party's responsibility to ask you.

SUCCESS LIES HIDDEN BEHIND THE CONFLICTS

- *Executing* any business plan basically involves the marrying of people to money.
- *Executing* always involves three steps: team building, budget allocation, and tactics formulation.
- East-West executing is made tougher because Cowboys and Dragons have such different traditions covering all three of these steps.
- The surest way to resolve the inevitable East-West *conflicts* is for each side to explain to the other side just *why* it does things the way it does. Then, the otherwise hidden motives for action become clear, and each conflict can be resolved in a joint manner.

RECOMMENDATIONS

1. *The cautionary rule.* Never assume that your Chinese counterparts do things the way you do. *Explain* how you build a team, obtain money, and run a business *before* you begin each of these steps. *Listen* to how your counterparts execute the same steps. Then, get flexible.
2. *Turf wars.* Cowboys *expect* to fight over management turf—and win. In the East, the moment you begin to fight, you have already lost. Dragons want common ground, not private turf. Respect that.
3. *The responsibility rule.* Each country has a responsibility rule, but the two rules are different. Cowboys say, "If you want to know how I do things, ask." Dragons say, "How are we going to do this thing?"

When you work with the Chinese, you must change the Cowboy rule and explain how you do things before you ever begin. Dragons won't ask! That would show disrespect and threaten *mainzi.*

EXPATRIATES

A REALITY LESSON

Internal compromises always spill over to cause external conflicts.

"I've got to convince my board that I've hired competent people." WSL Corporation completed several Chinese joint ventures around 1994 (companies and names have been changed). Its Asian Operations VP, Gary Cooper, had felt pushed into appointing Americans as venture leaders, overriding Chinese objections in five out of six instances. All the deals failed, except the one venture headed by a local Chinese executive.

It had seemed logical to appoint Chinese-Americans to these positions—after all, they knew Chinese language and culture, and also knew about *guanxi.* WSL had recruited technically competent Chinese-American engineers from companies like IBM. A big plus, these guys could also speak English and make great presentations to the parent company. The WSL Board readily rubber-stamped their appointments. What went wrong?

First, the Americans rode roughshod over Chinese sensibilities during the execution phase; local Chinese lost *mainzi* and became uncooperative. Second, the Chinese don't regard Chinese-Americans highly: "Fake Americans pretending to know Chinese." WSL had also selected technical people who possessed no business skills. Third, the American executive had yielded to *internal* company pressure. Ignore your partner's wishes only at your peril.

The Lesson: Expatriates can become a problem, not a solution, as joint venture leaders. The rule doesn't apply to wholly owned subsidiaries, where both Americans and expatriates can work out well.

CHAPTER NINETEEN

The Nine Most Likely
Points of Conflict and
How to Resolve Them

JUST BEFORE THE BANQUET

Just before the big celebration banquet began, a little "glitch" arose. Our Chinese host told the restaurant staff to hold off serving the food for just a little while. Once the small disagreement between the management groups representing WSL and the Chinese SSTIC got settled, we would all begin eating. Thirty-six hours later, we did.

The banquet had been scheduled for the formal signing of a joint venture agreement in a festive setting. After some 18 months of hard work, the basic decision to move forward had been reached and the execution plan agreed on. The leader for each party had arrived—Chairman Liu for SSTIC and Gary Cooper for WSL. Nobody expected a showdown at the OK corral.

Then someone raised a few minor points about capital contribution and return on investment (ROI) as well as the marketing budget. Big mistake. Minor points quickly escalated into a major disagreement. The joint negotiating team reassembled to iron things out. In the heat of the argument, they forgot how to work together and took sides. At the very last moment before the signing, neither side would give in.

Several hours passed with no resolution. Then the chief Chinese negotiator, GU Peide, a hard-core Communist technocrat, joined in. Both sides dug in their heels even more. The Cowboys argued "the numbers"; the Dragons argued that many Chinese could become offended if they gave in. Despite everything I could do, Mr. Gu in particular became more and more upset, particularly with me. Twenty-four hours had passed. The food staff still waited!

Then Mr. Gu's frustration boiled over: He shouted at me in a loud, angry voice, "I've seen many of *your* kind of Chinese-American. You are disguised as a Chinese, but you are trying to help the Americans." Now, I am normally very diplomatic, but right then I lost control of myself: "And *you* are a very strange kind of Chinese," I shouted back, "who refuses to understand the other side. No wonder you are unable to reach an agreement with the foreigners!" He felt chastised for a lack of hospitality.

> Dragons learn the art of indirect politeness from birth; they can, however, be *very* direct at times!

Our angry exchange worked like a thunderstorm, releasing a lot of pent-up emotion. After suitable apologies, we once more worked as a single team. The hot-button issues gradually got resolved. The restaurant staff then served up a splendid banquet.

THE HIERARCHIES OF CONCERN

Why did we experience such conflict? The underlying cause comes from our dissimilar and inverted hierarchies of concerns. The Cowboy hierarchy designates the more individual concerns as top priorities and then descends to more general concerns. The Dragon hierarchy places cooperative concerns at the top and descends to more narrow concerns. The two look like the inverted pyramids in Figure 19.1. In the two hierarchies, each side shares four similar basic concerns but prioritizes them differently. Our gut-felt issues don't line up.

FIGURE 19.1   Hierarchies of Concerns: East and West

Priority Level	West	East
A. Highest	The firm	Overall "social-political condition"
B. Second	The business deal	*Guanxi* relationships
C. Third	Interpersonal relations	Business proposition
D. Fourth	The "Free Enterprise System"	*Danwei*

Cowboys care most about immediate self-interest—making the company come out ahead. That is the Dragons' lowest concern. Always present at a visceral level, Cowboys underpin everything with loyalty to the free enterprise system—the system that allows them to put the firm at the top of the hierarchy. Dragons make their social system their highest concern and place their own *danwei* dead last. In between, business and relationship concerns have an inverted order as well. *At any given level in the hierarchy, the concerns will conflict.* Whenever either side argues from the standpoint of its own priorities, conflicts become inevitable.

THE NINE MOST LIKELY POINTS OF CONFLICT

Reading across the lines on the hierarchies of concerns in Figure 19.1, the most likely conflicts emerge as mismatches between priorities—some having a fairly obvious basis, some having sources hidden to the parties involved. The more hidden conflicts appear starred below; every one of the nine conflicts that follows comes directly from the inverted priorities that we each give to the same basic concerns.

Highest-level concerns (firm versus country):

1. *Corporate self-interest versus the good of the collective.* The "social-political condition" has an almost mystical importance to Dragons, very much in the way that Cowboys venerate "free enterprise." Cowboys expect to hammer out an agreement over what each side's company will get from the deal; Dragons see this behavior as a fundamental affront to country and culture.

2. *Free trade versus self-sufficiency.* Free enterprise Cowboys come to trade—trade anything so long as the company benefits. Cowboys utterly fail to recognize that the term *free trade* recalls coerced trade from the Chinese perspective. Beginning with the Opium War, the West forced a weak China into "unfair" trading arrangements. Cowboys see trading technology for markets as an "opening" into China. Dragons want the technology to become once more a single large workhouse supplying the whole country. They still dream of an insular China before the fall to the Western barbarians.

3. *Profit versus national employment.* Cowboys always preach great profits for both sides; Dragons hear "exploitation." Cowboys want "cheap labor"; Dragons find that offensive to their national pride but still want to keep all their people employed.

Second-level concerns (discrete business deal versus long-term relationships):

4. *The stand-alone deal versus a web of interconnected relations.* Cowboys deal for immediate private gain; Dragons regard the well-being of all work units related to their own *danwei*—a little like the American divisionalized corporation, wherein each operating division has some concern for the well-being of the other divisions.

5. *Individual product markets versus harmony of common needs.* Cowboys want to develop Chinese product markets; Dragons want to ensure that harmony prevails by meeting the common needs of all the people, beginning with the most basic.

Third-level concerns (business relationship versus the business proposition):

6. **Business growth versus long-term viability.* The Cowboy business mantra is growth; Cowboys place business relationships in the context of growing a business. Dragons want assurance that anything they agree to offers long-term viability; failures threaten *mainzi* and *danwei* as well as the social-political condition.

7. *Acquaintances versus institutional security.* Cowboys expect to make and lose many acquaintances as a business grows; Dragons desire institutional security and thus surround themselves with *guanxi* friendships as a part of *danwei.*

Fourth-level concerns (free enterprise versus the individual work unit):

8. **Survival of the fittest versus* danwei *and the single workhouse.* Cowboys are Darwinians at heart, Cowboys Marxists. Cowboys believe that only the strong survive; nice guys finish last. Dragons can envision all China as one vast workhouse, or collective, and their own *danwei* as a microcosm of their whole world.

9. *Consumption versus production.* Cowboys fear there won't be enough demand within the free enterprise system, so they wish to capture Chinese demand. Dragons are all producers in the workhouse; they want to keep every worker busy.

202 Cowboys and Dragons

The Parable of the Fly and the Bee: Both insects fly into an open bottle whose bottom points toward the light. Which insect escapes the bottle trap? The fly, who buzzes every which way. The bee steadfastly flies toward the light and remains trapped. Which insect resembles the Cowboys and which the Dragons?

RESOLVING CONFLICTS BEFORE AND AFTER THEY BEGIN

Every conflict can potentially be defused before it ever gets started through the art of *why.* For example, a Cowboy can anticipate Dragon high-level concerns about "greedy profits" and the "social-political condition" and explain to his Chinese counterpart why the American free enterprise system forces each American company to pursue its own welfare. Then the two leaders can explain their different basic economic systems to one another. Or a Cowboy can explain how modern international trade makes all countries better off when each country specializes in what it does best. In these examples, Cowboys and Dragons invoke the same, broad concerns based in political economy. *Explain, explain: Don't assume that the other side shares your priorities.*

When a conflict does erupt, where does it come from? In the example of the 36-hour marathon, one trigger was a mismatch between American desires for a substantial marketing budget and Chinese concern for waste in the "social-political condition": A second-level American concern triggered a highest-level Chinese one. By arguing from "the numbers" for a certain ROI—an American highest-level priority—the Cowboys again triggered highest-level Dragon concerns about exploitation. The stakes suddenly rose to great importance—conflicting highest-level priorities. *Resolving conflicts calls for answering the other side's concerns.*

The way you get treated in the East depends on what the other side wants. Cowboys call this "enlightened self-interest."

The conflicts got resolved only when the Cowboys pointed out that the American government would not support them if they failed in business. A certain ROI wasn't exploitation; it was necessary to preserve the American *danwei* and the long-term viability of the joint venture itself. That relieved some hidden Dragon concerns. The marketing budget would help the Chinese people understand a new product that would eventually be good for everyone—a highest-level Dragon concern. American and Chinese concerns now became closely aligned. The deal and the long-term relationship both got salvaged.

CONFLICTS COME FROM MISMATCHED PRIORITIES, NOT DIFFERENT NEEDS

- We all share similar, culturally defined *concerns.* Concerns run from our own personal ones to those for our overall society's well-being. Cowboys and Dragons just happen to assign *different priorities* to similar concerns.
- *Conflicts* arise out of differently prioritized concerns, not out of fundamental human differences. We all need the same basic things.
- *Conflicts can be avoided* when both sides *anticipate* the other's priorities and explain themselves in terms of the other party's culturally defined concerns. This can be quite difficult, because many conflicts arise out of hidden concerns that neither party may be aware of. When you thoroughly understand both the other party's culture, and your own, you will become able to identify hidden concerns.
- *Conflicts can get resolved* when each side answers the other's concerns.

RECOMMENDATIONS

1. *Irreconcilable differences?* There is no such thing as an irreconcilable difference. There are only basic needs, or concerns, and how we rank them. When a cross-cultural business conflict erupts, ask yourself the question: "What deep-seated need held by the other party have I exposed?" Then find a way to remove the threat.
2. *When to resolve conflicts.* It's always better to resolve a conflict *before* it even begins! You can often do this when you understand *who* the other party is and *why* it has particular, culturally defined concerns. In the East, a "true friend" is one who anticipates your concerns before you even voice them.
3. *After-the-fact conflict resolution.* Get the negatives out first; have *both* sides develop a list of them. This has the side benefit of defusing

emotions. Then have both sides list the positives—why we both wanted the venture in the first place. Last, reassure your counterparts about the perceived negatives; where possible, convert them into positives. (A bit of practical psychology: If you list the positives first, the negatives may overwhelm them, and you will lose the whole venture.)

PART SIX

What the Future Holds

For better or for worse, the United States and China have entered into a commercial common law marriage arrangement! We have lived too long totally apart, and now we will come more and more together. What will result from this "marriage of convenience"?

We may expect changes for the better in both country's political economies—those relations between governments and economies that generate the wealth of nations. Those changes in turn may bring our two business models into closer harmony. This won't happen purely by chance: both Cowboys and Dragons have intended this convergence. We won't become like two peas in a pod, however; we will each keep our own cultural identities. Cowboys will remain Cowboys, and Dragons will still be Dragons, but we *will* become friends.

CHAPTER TWENTY

An East-West Model
for Success

It was the best of times; it was the worst of times.
—A TALE OF TWO CITIES

Things united too long will split; things split too long will reunite.
—SAN GUO YAN YI
(THE STORY OF THREE KINGDOMS)

THE JOURNEY FROM AT&T TO NEUSTAR

AT&T faced a crisis in the 1980s culminating in the historic court action that broke up a long-term, government-granted monopoly. The breakup created revolutionary opportunities for many companies—both new hardware providers and long-distance service providers. Real competition among long-distance providers required number portability, however—the ability for customers to retain their telephone numbers while changing long-distance providers. Capitalism is creative destruction.

In 1999, a company called NeuStar won a Federal Communications Commission (FCC) contract to provide telephone number management services for the whole nation (see the NeuStar case study). NeuStar now seeks to become the *global* provider of this critical service. What the American courts tore asunder, customer need has brought back together, in a totally new structure. As a Cowboy might put it: What comes around goes around.

WAY GI

One of the West's favorite novels, by Charles Dickens, begins: "It was the best of times; it was the worst of times." Perhaps the most popular book in Chinese history, *San Guo Yan Yi (The Story of Three Kingdoms)*, begins with the characters meaning: "Things united too long will split; things split too long will reunite." Both sentences capture a sense for the dual nature of crisis: Danger and opportunity become handmaidens.

Opportunity consists of danger balanced by desire. No great action ever happens until desire wins out over danger.

Dickens directly expresses this sense of the dual possibilities present in a crisis. The Chinese version contains considerably more complexity, suggesting that change-bringing crises occur naturally over time, like *Tao*. Things remain eternally in a state of flux. Nothing exists in a steady state.

The Dickens quotation contains a very Western philosophical notion: The history of things develops in stages, a step-by-step progression. The Chinese quotation suggests a different, and less explicit, notion: Things occur rhythmically in cycles, not progressively. Stages are man driven; cycles occur as part of the natural order. A number of pictures can be conceived for what such cycles may look like: revolutions, expansions and contractions, and upward and downward spirals. Stages may very well exist within each cycle, but things always return to a former state.

In the West, all change appears linear; in the East, it appears cyclical.

The Chinese word for *crisis* contains that word's ambiguous nature within its characters. "Crisis" in Chinese is *way gi*. *Way* means "danger" or "fear." *Gi* means "opportunity" or "desire." Combined, the two characters suggest a repulsion-attraction conflict. Fear of danger pushes a person away from a crisis situation; desire for opportunity pushes that person forward into the situation. Every new venture brings out both human forces. Eventually, one natural force or the other wins out. Nothing stays stationary for long.

The AT&T story parallels the Chinese sense for how crises develop: Things united too long will split—as did AT&T in the government nut-cracker. Things divided too long will reunite—as such forces as number portability and broadband standards work themselves out within the information technology sector. The American equivalent of this thought uses the dual concept of bundling and unbundling, of both product attri-butes and companies themselves. The Chinese model is less practical but more philosophical and indirect—and perhaps more profound.

WESTERN AND EASTERN MODELS

Westerners and Easterners look outward through lenses focused by his-torical culture and see landscapes comprised of both cultural and material environments. The environments differ greatly. Although the focus here will be on business models, contrasting worldviews will always be very much in the immediate background. Environment matters more than genes.

The Western business model divides all aspects of a business plan into five functional areas: marketing/sales, technology/product development, operations/manufacturing, finance/accounting, and administration. More generally, the Western model creates firm boundaries: Business and gov-ernment are separate domains. Each and every institution has a border or frame around it, just as a Western painting has a frame: The frame contrib-utes to the art.

The East doesn't instinctively think in such terms, although many younger people in the East now possess American-style MBA degrees and know about these functional areas. Dragons perceive a world where the environment has not been chopped up into categories, just as Chinese art is frameless. The Western model is a triumph over what the Chinese still regard as a naturally occurring ebb and flow of affairs. For the East, the background possesses as much importance as the art objects in it.

The West follows function; the East follows nature.

THE MARKETING CONCEPT—NOT AS
UNIVERSAL AS YOU THINK

In Western business, a simple model ties all five functional areas together: Identify customer needs in order to offer products that satisfy
those needs. It seems so obvious, but the East doesn't naturally think
in such terms. So a typical misconnect between Cowboys and Dragons
goes something like this: An American executive says to his Chinese
counterpart, "Give me your market survey results." The Dragon replies,
"We don't have any market surveys. The government decides customer
needs." The Cowboy asks in bewilderment, "Then how can you know
what products to offer?" "Everybody needs the same things." It is just
like AT&T before the breakup!

THE TWO WORLDS OF R&D

Cowboys do a lot of new product research and development (R&D).
Because so much R&D in the West doesn't fall under government control,
a lot of duplicated effort always occurs. Several American corporations
may work on the same basic technology at the same time, producing a
number of slightly different answers to the same basic need. Dragons
regard such activity as very wasteful: why not have just one organization
doing this work? Of course, before the breakup, exactly such a situation
existed for the American telecom industry. AT&T once told us all what we
needed: not very much. Until the 1950s, Americans couldn't even get col-
ored telephones.

In China, the bulk of the research gets done by one organization—the
government. The government then tries to get businesses to do the development work. It has not worked out very well. Similarly, Bell Labs used
to produce great basic research, but AT&T business units didn't do a good
job of developing research into new products. China looks like the old
AT&T!

R&D has an empirical nature—trial and error. The more trials performed, the more likely a successful outcome will appear. So the West,
with its multiple, "wasteful" R&D projects, has yielded better results
overall. Might there be a better way than either?

WORLDS OF DIFFERENCE

The differences continue for operations, finance, and administration. The West has learned to apply man-made systems to *operations.* The Chinese have for some time been eager to learn these methods. From a broader perspective, the West has created the bureaucratic structure, whether in business, education, or government. The Chinese *danwei* model, on the other hand, has an organic rather than a systematic nature and perhaps possesses more flexibility and adaptability. Might the two somehow come closer together?

Western *finance* has created an entirely new management field—the control of risk. Risk management is new to the Chinese who still think largely in terms of managing social harmony. Dragons still see the world of money in zero-sum terms: There is only so much, and it must be carefully spread around to where it will do the most social good. Cowboys understand that wealth gets created, perhaps the most basic conclusion reached by modern Western economics that began with Adam Smith. Thus, Dragons conserve wealth from the past, whereas Cowboys create new wealth and leverage it for the future. Distributing created wealth more equitably, however, remains the challenge for the West; creating more wealth in the first place remains the challenge for the East.

Cowboy *administration* is decisive. One Cowboy makes the call for a whole company compared with Chinese decision making by consensus. Consensus has a way of avoiding major pitfalls—danger—but also missing out on opportunity. Both Cowboys and Dragons sense that certain times are better than others for opportunity taking. Cowboys talk about getting the timing right for a new undertaking; Dragons sense that a time exists for action and a time for inaction. Timing for Cowboys stands as an analytical idea. The right time for Dragons follows the natural flow of powerful positive and negative forces. The right time for East and West to form a new relation appears to be right now.

Cowboys are goal people, whereas Dragons are river people—they go with the flow.

THE MIDDLE WAY

For many years, Western countries tried to force China and the rest of the East into the Western model—an attempt that reached a climax in the 1898 Boxer Rebellion. Japan likewise tried to conquer China for the Greater Co-Prosperity Sphere. At each of these turning points, China resisted intrusion. Now, another turning point has arisen, but this time not from physical force. China, after all, has chosen to enter the World Trade Organization (WTO) and to host the 2008 Summer Olympics. How shall the East and the West deal with each other in the near future?

The middle way appears central to both Confucian and Greek thought and may resolve East-West conflicts. The middle way won't absorb one culture into the other, either peaceably or by force. Instead, elements of both models will combine, with business leading the way. The new reality will be a mosaic, not a melting pot where one side melds into the other.

> The mosaic, not the melting pot, will symbolize the new meeting of East and West.

Nothing better symbolizes the new opportunities for East-West cooperation than the simple eye contact story in Chapter 1. In that story, Cowboy and Dragon business leaders failed to form a relationship, symbolized by failed eye contact, because of their basic cultural differences. However, once Dragons learn that American direct eye contact communicates "I am paying attention" and Cowboys learn that Chinese looking aside communicates respect, each can relate to, and learn from, the other. A new civility has been conceived.

SHIFTING BOUNDARIES AND INITIATIVES

What might the middle way look like in future business practice? One large area will involve *consumer/customer needs*. Western consumer needs now exist largely unbounded, whereas Chinese customer needs still remain largely a dictate of government. Let's look at a possible middle way. In the West and East alike, governments will make certain assumptions about people's overall welfare needs through democratic processes. Business entities will survey consumers to verify the assumptions. Such a consultation process will yield bounded opportunities for business.

Consultation will replace warfare in the West and a dictatorship of choice in China.

The term *warfare* may seem jarring. Consider, however, how America has dealt with significant *public health and environmental issues* to date, issues that inevitably yield more bounded business realities. Asbestos and tobacco litigation has forced boundaries on business through legal combat. Trial lawyers have become either white knights or black villains depending on your point of view. Fast food appears to be the next target for combat. The first lawsuit against fast-food firms for "causing" a man's obesity has already begun in litigious New York City.

Environmental protection remains a mixture of legal actions and government-imposed regulations. Meanwhile, America has spent far more on legal fees than on cleanup costs. Eventually, government legislation will replace the inefficiencies of trial by lawyers. Business will have a consultative role in boundary setting, just as special interest groups now do, and the end result will be a bounded reality that businesses may innovate within. Reverse the direction, and the process within China appears. East and West come together.

The matter of *technological development* may also follow a course to a middle way where government and business form a more unified and bounded approach to change. This has happened already and continues to happen with regard to the Internet. I participated in some of the earliest work on what has become the Internet while at Univac in the late 1960s. The overall effort became ARPANet and met military needs. ARPANet technology then extended to academia. It didn't develop commercial applications until the early 1990s, some 25 years after government began it. Government, then, initiated the most liberating device on planet Earth!

Overall, government has provided the Internet framework of rules, just as it has for telecommunications and information technology more generally, and the rules provide a relatively safe, bounded reality for business product development. The Internet combines elements of East and West, and offers a good model for future technology development efforts (see the next case study for a look inside WWW.R&D).

It is fundamentally true that things too long united will split, and things too long divided will reunite. The immediate future leads down a pathway bringing East and West closer together, but inevitably the paths will diverge again, and each world—composed of Cowboys and Dragons—will reclaim something of its own traditional identity. In the meantime, we will all become much better off for going through this latest natural cycle.

THINGS SPLIT TOO LONG WILL COME TOGETHER

- *Crisis* always contains elements of both danger and opportunity. Eventually one or the other force swings us out of crisis, but progressive change happens only when the desire for opportunity consistently overweighs the fear of danger. Crises always come before great positive advances.
- Even though *steps* exist along the way to any significant change, change itself follows a cyclical pathway in which crises and resolutions of crises follow one another. Things too long united will split, and things too long divided will reunite. In Western philosophical terms, this is all very Hegelian.
- The ongoing crises between East and West will resolve themselves into a new *middle way* that will contain the most valuable elements of both worlds without destroying the fundamental cultural natures of either. The result will be a new global mosaic, not a single world culture. We won't all blend together!
- *The business middle way.* A new model for business success combining elements of both East and West is quietly emerging. It will consist of a new balance between opposing forces: *government boundaries and corporate initiative.* I predict that a new balance between these two forces will produce more profitable and less risky business ventures in the future—both national and international in scope.

RECOMMENDATIONS FOR DEALING WITH GLOBAL CHANGE

1. *Way gi.* Change always has two sides: danger and opportunity. It is somewhat like standing behind an elephant; from that angle, it is difficult to see the advantages the elephant offers. As a businessperson, look for the opportunities. Dangers will take care of themselves.
2. *Get to know the other world.* Once you know who the people of the East are, they will seem far less dangerous.
3. *Become an earthling.* When I talk to business students, I always recommend that they study and strive to be less completely Western or Eastern and more citizens of the world—*earthlings.* None of us can become earthlings completely, but the journey is worth the effort, personally and professionally.

NEUSTAR

GLOBAL IT
REVOLUTION IN THE MAKING

Jeff Ganek joined Lockheed-Martin (LM) in 1995 as a senior vice president in its Information Management Services (IMS) Division. IMS evolved from strictly military information services into business information services as well. Jeff headed up the business-related unit, which became involved in developing telephone number administration software for the American telecom industry. By 1999, Jeff's unit had received tentative FCC approval for its software and had the opportunity to become the nation's single private contractor providing number administration. Only one hang-up, the FCC wouldn't award the contract to a nondedicated supplier such as Lockheed-Martin. In order to gain the contract, the unit would have to get spun off.

From 1995 onward, Jeff had been growing increasingly dissatisfied with corporate life. Since meeting at AT&T, we had become friends in the Eastern sense of the word. I advised him to avoid any further big company involvement, and when the spin-off became a real possibility, we talked about how he could acquire his unit and found his own firm, soon named NeuStar. With FCC approval, in December 1999 NeuStar acquired the LM assets necessary to become the nation's only number administrator. We raised $19 million through Warburg Princus to finance the deal.

NeuStar solved the number portability problem arising in the wake of the AT&T breakup. Meaningful long-distance carrier competition required the capability for users to switch service providers while retaining their same telephone numbers and avoiding the use of clumsy special access codes. All U.S. telecom companies signed on with NeuStar for a five-year contract period. Soon, Canada joined as well, creating NAMPA (North American Number Planning Administration). The next year, NeuStar made impressive gains in Europe, adding eight countries of the European Union to its system.

The potential for centralized and *global* information management goes beyond what NeuStar has achieved to date—in two areas: merging telecom and Internet information and bringing Asia into the overall management system. NeuStar has already begun undertaking strategic actions in both areas. Recently, the firm acquired the domain name rights to both dot-biz and dot-US. Dot-biz creates a whole new business domain facilitating e-business activity; and dot-US brings U.S. domain names in line with other countries. NeuStar will next combine telecom numbers and Internet addresses into one extremely powerful database.

In April of 2001, when Jeff asked me to help NeuStar enter Asian telecom markets, I agreed. I'm sure neither one of us had any idea when we met back in 1985 how far our personal *guanxi* would take us. Together we have lived through the breakup of a vast telecom monopoly, and now we are working together to create a new convergence of the globally disparate parts to both telecoms and the Internet. *Things split too long will reunite.*

Things united too long will split. The Internet has become a global information superhighway — truly the new Silk Road, as NeuStar executives recognize. Since the Internet became an international phenomenon, however, a new problem has emerged: the "Digital Divide." Internet-related access and fluency have become the latest separators of the world's rich and poor. Information yields power, and power breeds wealth.

Alphabets and languages, in turn, have become major contributors to the international digital divide. Ninety percent of the world's people possess a mother tongue other than English; soon, two-thirds of all Internet users will be non-English speakers. And most of the non-Western world doesn't use the Roman alphabet. Recently, new browser software supporting non-Roman fonts, such as Chinese, Japanese, and Arabic, has alleviated the alphabet problem. Domain names — Web site addresses — remain exclusively in the Roman alphabet, however, and domain names provide the locations on the Internet's virtual world map. The tyranny of ASCII code makes World Wide Web addresses look like gobbledygook for maybe half the world's people!

The problem, it turns out, isn't technical: Superlanguages — superset translators really — can potentially provide everyone on earth readable domain names without translating them into every language on earth. A multilingual domain names system, or MDNS, has recently been demonstrated. The problem, instead, appears *political and cultural.* The Internet has forced both East and West into a state of rapid and irreversible transition; the only question is where the transition will lead. Here, MINC comes in.

MINC stands for Multilingual Internet Names Consortium. Its founders, who are largely Asians, wish to implement MDNS globally. They need to find a way to become understood by Internet Corporation for Assigned Names and Numbers (ICANN), the centralized international organization that controls several important technical functions keeping the World Wide Web running including basic protocols for domain names. The West has developed a technology truly global in scope; now we need to learn how to effectively share it with the East. If we don't, then the Web can never be truly "World Wide." Domain names stand for all of the conflicts East and West have faced for centuries. The matter of Cowboys versus Dragons underlies even the digital divide.

Recently the Vice Chairman of MINC, Professor TAN Tin Wee, spoke with me in Singapore about MINC's need for someone who completely understands both the East and the West. He even tried to recruit me to head up MINC: "Charles, you can quote both *The Story of the Three Kingdoms* and Dickens! The people of the East have become so frustrated," he told me. "There is a cry among Asians for Westerners to understand us. We know the Americans; they don't know us." A single, centralized organization has for too long dominated domain names with an outmoded model that disregards over half the world's needs.

Simultaneously, global information technology forces are bringing together user information too long kept apart, while driving apart Westernized addresses kept too long together in one model. No other set of global phenomena better illustrates these two tendencies, or natural forces, than NeuStar and MINC. Will the day come when every citizen of Planet Earth has his or her own unique number—globally transportable—that provides total information access in a comprehensible superlanguage set for telecom and Internet? I think so.

CHAPTER TWENTY-ONE

By Chance or Design?

May you live through interesting times.
—AN OLD CHINESE PROVERB

When I speak before business school classes, I often ask students in closing a seemingly simple question: "Did we meet here today by chance, or by design?" Almost everybody answers, "By chance." I answer, "By design. We both designed to meet here today."

It may be that our first meeting comes about seemingly by chance: You stumble into class and find me there. Our next meeting, however, almost always comes about by design: You and I both choose whether the next meeting happens. Perhaps you wish to learn more about venture capital or doing business with Pacific Rim countries. Then the first meeting appears to be something more than a random event; it takes on the nature of serendipity—an aptitude for making fortuitous discoveries accidentally. Some reason comes into our shared vision for meeting again. Nothing happens by pure chance.

WHAT DESIGN LOOKS LIKE

If we meet by design, by choice, what does that look like? What sort of intelligence brought it about? First, design in this regard resembles a story, not a structure. The initial two parts to the story we know already: We met by design, not by chance, and now we both choose to continue our relationship. Each of us now acts out a script; our two scripts combined create the plot line for the story. How one person's script interacts with another's determines our "fate." Fate merely constitutes interactions of life scripts; random events become the joker thrown into the deck to make things interesting.

Scripts have great importance, but who writes them? Only two possibilities exist: either you write your own, or somebody else writes it for you. The chief contracted outside script writers happen to be parents and teachers along with spouses and children—and our *danwei* superiors. When you write your own script, it looks very much like a business plan; it contains goals, strategy, an execution plan, and tactics. When somebody writes it for you, it looks like a jumble of cultural preconceptions— a Cowboy script or a Dragon script.

If you wish to write your own script, what sort of intelligence will you need? The question strikes Cowboys and Dragons alike as rather absurd. Only one sort of intelligence exists, each will tell you. In reality, both use different forms of intelligence to arrive at the same answer! Cowboys emphasize rational intelligence; Dragons emphasize emotional intelligence. The two intelligences bring us back to where this book began— with Mars and Venus. Cowboys are men; Dragons are women. Cowboys tend toward rational thinking; Dragons tend toward emotional intuiting. The script has changed from one described by Dr. John Gray to one described by Daniel Goleman in his best-seller *Emotional Intelligence:* Successful scripts come from men and women, East and West, who use emotional intelligence to execute rational planning.

Emotional intelligence has several domains—the most important one here being handling relationships. Emotionally smart people create, nurture, and harvest relationships.

Mars and Venus showed us how very different Cowboys and Dragons really are. Emotional intelligence shows us our common, underlying similarity; it determines success far more than does rational intelligence— and everyone on Planet Earth either has emotional intelligence or can learn it. For East and West to successfully meet in the future, each needs to develop the aspect of emotional intelligence that furthers relationships with the other. Emotional intelligence is the design tool for *guanxi* and planned-out life scripts alike.

Life-scripted *guanxi* has such importance that it can be regarded as a *third intelligence*—interpersonal intelligence. People who learn this intelligence can form groups, negotiate between groups or within groups, and

> The domain of rational intelligence is things. The domain of emotional intelligence is persons. Never confuse the two.

create multiple interpersonal connections, all to reach life goals. A common thread runs through all of these actions: harmony. This is very Eastern. Blessed are the peacemakers. That is very Western.

The future will bring us closer together as we attach more importance to all of these intelligences. Western rational thinking has cracked open the mysteries of the world and the universe. Eastern emotional thinking has generated large-scale social harmony. Interpersonal intelligence has created remarkable human group achievements. In the future, Cowboys will place more emphasis on emotional and interpersonal intelligences, and Dragons will do the same for rational intelligence. We will still have very different cultures, but we will each benefit from our relationship with the other.

Visible and Invisible Hands

Design also matters on a larger scale—the scale of political economy. Here, the East-West situation flips. The West emphasizes markets; the East has emphasized rational design. In reality, markets possess nonhuman design properties: spontaneous orderliness. Just as in the personal case, nothing happens by pure chance. In markets, spontaneously occurring events yield serendipitous order, something very Eastern in its sensibility. Human intelligence yields the corporation or the *danwei*, which also yields order. That is very Western. One works as if by an *invisible hand*, as Adam Smith expressed it; the other works by the *visible hand* (as Chairman Mao might have said but didn't). In the future, East and West will learn to combine the invisible and visible hands to design better economies.

> The classic book on human organizations is Alfred Chandler's *Visible Hand*. You may wish to have a look at it.

Guanxi: Designed In

Guanxi may still seem inscrutable to Western eyes. It shouldn't. Guanxi is rationally designed by each creator of it and follows design rules: First, guanxi grows by following opportunity; second, it gets built over time by using integrity—that is, mainzi emotional intelligence—in its construction. Guanxi must grow by the purposeful pursuit of gain through opportunity, because no one has unlimited time and energy to expend, and both time and energy are necessary for guanxi to exist at all. Guanxi demands interpersonal intelligence and consists of long-term personal capital development.

When you have built up a guanxi emotional bank account, you may then freely make withdrawals from it. When he founded NeuStar and when he approached me about NeuStar in Asia, Jeff Ganek made some guanxi withdrawals from his bank account. They have paid off. Emotional bank accounts, or guanxi obligations, will matter more and more as East and West develop mutual harmony.

THINGS ALWAYS END WITH A QUESTION

Tell me now, did you meet me in this book by chance or by design?

ABOUT EVOLUTION AND DESIGN

- Nothing happens by chance.
- *Serendipity.* The aptitude for making fortuitous discoveries accidentally explains why some people appear luckier than others as their life scripts play out.
- *Multiple intelligences.* Serendipity, in turn, involves using intelligences beyond the merely *rational,* such as *emotional* and *interpersonal* intelligences.
- *Designed-in economics.* Whole economies possess innate "intelligence" in the form of spontaneous orderliness. Governments can rationally plan, but markets spontaneously evolve new orders of things.
- *Designed-in guanxi.* Guanxi also happens by design through interpersonal intelligence. How big is your emotional bank account with other people?

RECOMMENDATIONS

1. *Write your own life script.* The road to happiness never follows someone else's design for you. Who has designed your life script?
2. *Create your own luck.* If you use interpersonal intelligence to build up your own *guanxi* bank account, serendipitous good things will begin to happen for you that would never otherwise come into existence. There is really no such thing as luck—only design.
3. *If you want something, ask for it.* You will receive.

APPENDIX

QUICK TIPS FOR NAVIGATING CHINESE BUSINESS AND STREET CULTURE

- *Food.* The Chinese always think of *Chinese* food when they host you for a meal. It's OK to suggest to your Chinese hosts that *you* host them at a Western restaurant for a change. At a Chinese restaurant, indicate what dishes you want; and ask for a knife and fork if chopsticks baffle you.
- *Seating at meals.* Your host sits at the table's head. At a round table, the head is opposite the door. The guest of honor sits at the right side of the host, and the second most important guest to the left. Thereafter, seating follows the *danwei* pecking order. At a round table, the least important person in the host's party sits in front of the doorway.
- *A tip.* In Hong Kong and many mainland restaurants, your bill includes a 10 percent service charge for management. You should tip your wait staff 5 to 8 percent more if the service is good. Hotel busboys expect $1 to $2 *per bag*—a pretty good job in the East.
- *Courtesy.* A wrong part of American culture says that it is all right to treat service people or others below us rudely so long as we say "please." The Chinese have great sensitivity to impoliteness and become readily offended. If in doubt, treat an older Chinese person the way you would your own father or mother, and a younger adult the way you would your grown son or daughter.
- *Dress.* Traditional Chinese emphasize comfort over style; for younger Chinese, fashion matters more. For everyone, drab Mao uniforms are out; Western-style business suits are in. Older Chinese wear looser-fitting suits, but everyone likes good style and color coordination.

You cannot go wrong wearing a suit and tie. Overdress rather than underdress. Choose conservative and proper styles. Don't dress down to look like some older Chinese.

- *Meeting protocol.* The Chinese boss always walks first, coming or going. Only the Number One person speaks. If he or she is absent, Number Two does all the talking. Seating assignments at rectangular tables always place the heads of the two delegations across from one another at the center of the two sides. The Chinese traditionally bow to each other when meeting but not as stiffly as the Japanese; juniors bow lower than seniors. Handshaking has become common.
- *Addressing one another.* The Chinese address one another by family name and title—no first names. Address a Chinese counterpart as "Mr. (last name)" or "Minister (last name)." You won't get on a first-name basis with your Chinese counterparts for a long time. The Chinese don't have Western-style "buddies."
- *Names.* Every Chinese has a last or family name, which always appears first, and a given name; no middle names. Asking someone Chinese to repeat his or her name is pleasing, because it shows interest and respect. As an illustration of a Chinese name, consider my own: LEE Tsung-Nan. Lee is my family name. Given names in China are chosen by parents and traditionally have two characters. In my case, Tsung is a family generational name that follows genealogy, and Nan is a character that my parents chose. It turns out that Tsung-Nan was a well-known general of my father's generation as well as an acquaintance of his, so I received his given name.
- *Chinese and Japanese names.* You can always tell the two apart, because Chinese last names are always single syllable words, whereas Japanese last names are always multiple syllable words.
- *Timeliness.* Be a little early arriving at appointments, and expect Chinese elevators to run more slowly! It's always better that you wait than that your host waits.
- *Business cards.* Don't leave home without them! Exchanging cards is an important introductory ritual. Present and receive cards with both hands to show respect, and read cards when you receive them.
- *Hotel accommodations.* Hotel accommodations are generally excellent in the coastal cities and in Beijing. Five-star hotel chains such as Hyatt and Hilton have signature facilities in Beijing and major coastal cities. The best Chinese hotels offer the services normally available in America, but if you travel inland, expect hotel quality to decline.

- *The energy saver.* Many Chinese hotel rooms have energy-saver master electrical switches. To get light, stick your room key or card in the master slot.
- *Private accommodations.* Don't expect your host to invite you to his home. Only honored friends receive such treatment. Most private dwellings are still of low quality by Western standards; only the corrupt live opulently. Most housing is still in apartment blocks, not freestanding. *Avoid small talk about housing!* Above all, don't commit the social gaffe of asking questions about your hosts' homes. Cowboy tall talk about big houses and stories meant to one-up the other guy are absolute no-nos. (If you invite your Chinese counterparts to America, do ask them to your own home, not to show off but to show intimacy and that you are becoming friends.)
- *Transportation.* Air travel between coastal cities is easy and convenient. Most Chinese travel by train. If you do so, book first-class soft-seat sleeper sections only. Coastal travel by train is perfectly safe, but it could be dangerous in some inland areas.
- *Personal space.* Westerners need a lot of personal space; Chinese very little. Expect the Chinese to converse with you as close as a foot away. Same-sex touching is quite common for the younger generation.
- *Courtesy.* Courtesy and patience always produce results in China, where anger and temper fail.
- *The art of listening.* Your counterpart will use many words; try to determine which are important, and listen for what has *not* been said.
- *Smile a lot.* A smile can work wonders with local officials.
- *Expect some body contact.* In public places, you will be brushed aside and even pushed. It is not rude to do the same; the Chinese have no concept of private personal space surrounding them. The Chinese don't queue up in lines for service as a rule; whoever gets a server's attention gets served.
- *Don't drink tap water!* Only the best hotels have potable water. (At home, Chinese boil drinking water, which is called "cool boiled water.") Pure bottled water is readily available. Use it. Ice cubes, where available, have been made from purified water.
- *Avoid public toilets and "street food."* Both may be very unsanitary. Remind yourself to use the facilities before leaving hotels and restaurants.
- *Bring along a roll.* If you go to out-of-the-way places, you will find toilet paper scarce.

BIBLIOGRAPHY

Cowboys and Dragons is not an academic book, and I am not a scholar, but I would like to mention just a few books that you may find helpful. In nearly all cases, they are titles that have come out recently and are readily available. I have found it helpful to categorize them as follows: Doing business in China today, Chinese-American comparative history and culture, Background on China, Background on Western civilization, and Chinese and Western developments in the applied sciences.

Doing Business in China Today

The most recent book in this category that I have read is by Professor Chen Ming-Jer entitled *Inside Chinese Business* (Cambridge: Harvard Business School Press, 2001). This very fine book gives the reader a lot of information about Chinese family businesses outside of mainland China, as well as about Chinese business culture and history. John Stuttard, a former PriceWaterhouse CEO, has written a very good book called *The New Silk Road: Secrets of Business Success in China Today* (New York: Wiley, 2000). The book uses material from actual interviews with 11 CEOs from international corporations doing business in China. *Doing Business in China* by Tim Ambler and Morgan Witzel (London: Routledge, 2000) give a lot of vital information about Chinese business practices, market conditions, negotiating, and business organizations. You may also find a new edition of the classic Chinese book on warfare very interesting because the author applies *The Art of War* to modern business situations. See *Sun Tzu's Art of War: The Modern Chinese Interpretation* by Tao Han-chang (New York: Sterling, 2000).

Chinese-American Comparative History and Culture

I have found only one book in this category that shows a mastery of both Chinese and American culture and history: *Americans and Chinese: Passages to Differences*, third edition, by Francis L.K. Hsu (Honolulu: University of Hawaii Press, 1981). This book is a must read.

Background on China

The most influential 20th-century Western scholar writing about China is John Fairbank of Harvard. His recent textbook brings together much of his 50 years' knowledge about the Middle Kingdom. It is titled *China: A New History* (Cambridge: Harvard University Press, 1998). This book will get you deeply into the subject, and point you toward many other books to read on a huge subject.

Background on Western Civilization

Several recently published books have made this overwhelming subject both comprehensible and fun. Charles Freeman updates the story of Classical Greece in *The Greek Achievement: The Foundation of the Western World* (London: Penguin, 2000). Two of Thomas Cahill's books do a highly creative job of shining new light on the beginnings of the Western mind and the preservation of ancient Western learning through the Dark Ages. They are: *The Gifts of the Jews: How a Tribe of Desert Nomads Changed the Way Everybody Thinks and Feels* (New York: Doubleday, 1998) and *How the Irish Saved Civilization: The Untold Story of Ireland's Heroic Role from the Fall of Rome to the Rise of Medieval Europe* (New York: Doubleday, 1995).

Chinese and Western Developments in the Applied Sciences

The modern authority on the history of Chinese science and technical innovation is Joseph Needham. His much longer original work has been reduced to only (!) three volumes, titled *The Shorter Science and Civilization in China* (New York: Cambridge University Press, 1978–1995). In the West, Roger Backhouse has just recently finished a remarkable book on the history of Western economics: *Ordinary Business of Life: A History of Economics from the Ancient World to the Twenty-First Century* (Princeton: Princeton

University Press, 2002). Of course, there is also that Western classic *The Wealth of Nations* (1776) by Adam Smith, available in many editions modern and old. This is one of those books you should read again—perhaps for the first time. A good complement to Adam Smith covering the "invisible hand" of the marketplace is Harvard Business School scholar Alfred Chandler's *Visible Hand: The Managerial Revolution in American Business* (Cambridge: Harvard University Press, 1980).

I have found three works of contemporary Western psychology that offer some insights into our cultural differences, and underlying similarities, East and West: *Men Are from Mars, Women from Venus* (New York: HarperCollins, 1992) by John Gray; *Emotional Intelligence: Why It Can Matter More Than IQ* (New York: Bantam, 1997) by Daniel Goleman; and *Games People Play: The Psychology of Human Relations* (New York: Random House 1996) by Eric Berne. Lastly, there is the Western classic in philosophy that can help us see how flat our cultural perspectives may be: *Flatland: A Romance of Many Dimensions* by Edwin A. Abbott (Cambridge, USA: Perseus, 2002).

Happy Reading!

INDEX

HOW'S YOUR *DANWEI?*

To get copies of
Cowboys and Dragons
for your whole organization,
please contact Mindi Rowland
in Special Sales,
800-621-9621, ext. 4410,
rowland@dearborn.com.

Your company also can order
Cowboys and Dragons with a
customized cover featuring
your name, logo, and message.

Dearborn™
Trade Publishing
A **Kaplan Professional** Company